The Entre

Min

Unleashing Your Inner Innovator and Building a Successful Venture

While every precaution has been taken in the preparation of this book, the publisher assumes no responsibility for errors or omissions, or for damages resulting from the use of the information contained herein.

THE ENTREPRENEURIAL MINDSET: BUILDING SUCCESS

First edition. November 28, 2023.

Copyright © 2023 imed el arbi.

ISBN: 979-8223425779

Written by imed el arbi.

The Entrepreneurial Mindset: Unleashing Your Inner Innovator and Building a Successful Venture

-

Understanding
the Entrepreneurial Mindset
What Entrepreneurship Is Not

The term "entrepreneurship" is frequently used in many different settings, but what does it actually mean? Fundamentally, entrepreneurship is the process of spotting possibilities, taking calculated chances, and adding value by developing and putting into practice novel concepts. It involves pursuing ideas with initiative, resourcefulness, and resilience in order to make them a reality.

The Entrepreneur's Role Entrepreneurs are essential to the expansion of the economy and the advancement of society. They are the agents of change, always looking for fresh approaches to issues, demands, and methods to enhance the quality of already-available goods, services, and procedures. Entrepreneurs have the ability to disrupt industries, create employment, and alter the future via taking

chances and embracing uncertainty.

The Mindset of an Entrepreneur

The entrepreneurial attitude is the foundation of entrepreneurship. The distinct mindset and problem-solving style of entrepreneurs distinguishes them from others. A person with an entrepreneurial mentality is able to recognize possibilities, take measured risks, and manage the challenges of launching and expanding a business. This is achieved by a mix of attributes, attitudes, and actions.

Important Components of the Entrepreneurial Mentality

1. zeal and goal

Entrepreneurs are motivated by a strong sense of purpose and a burning enthusiasm for their concepts. Their tenacity

1

and resolve in the face of challenges and disappointments are fueled by this passion. Entrepreneurs are able to encourage and inspire people to accompany them on their path because of their unshakeable faith in their goal.

Originality & Creativity

Entrepreneurs are naturally imaginative people with the capacity to think creatively and unconventionally in order to solve challenges. They are always looking for fresh approaches to develop completely new products or services or to enhance already-existing ones. They like change and don't hesitate to question the status quo.

Taking Chances and Being Strong

Entrepreneurs are willing to venture beyond of their comfort zones and are at ease with taking chances. They see failure as a chance to develop and learn, realizing that it's a necessary part of the entrepreneurial path. They are very resilient; they overcome adversity and turn it into a springboard for further achievement.

Flexibility and Adaptability

Entrepreneurs are adaptive and agile individuals who can swiftly modify their plans and tactics in reaction to unanticipated events or shifting market conditions. They welcome criticism and are always looking for methods to hone and polish their concepts and methods.

Inventiveness and Willpower

Resourceful people who know how to maximize scarce resources are considered entrepreneurs. They are adept at coming up with original answers to problems and do not let setbacks get to them down. They have a strong sense of purpose and are prepared to work hard and make the sacrifices necessary to see their ideas through to completion.

Different Kinds of Entrepreneurs

There are many different types of entrepreneurs, and each has a distinct combination of abilities, backgrounds, and driving forces. While some entrepreneurs are motivated by the possibility of financial gain and wealth creation, others are inspired by the desire to have a positive social effect and address urgent societal concerns. Whatever their reasons for starting a business, all of them want to add value and change the world.

Entrepreneurs with a Lifestyle

Entrepreneurs who launch enterprises exclusively to finance their ideal lifestyle are known as lifestyle entrepreneurs. They place more value on adaptability and independence than they do on quick development. In order to mix work and leisure in a way that best fits their lifestyle choices, lifestyle entrepreneurs frequently seek businesses that are in line with their own hobbies and passions.

Entrepreneurs in Social Media

The goal of bringing about constructive social change motivates social entrepreneurs. They see urgent societal problems and provide creative methods to deal with them. Social entrepreneurs are dedicated to improving the lives of others and are driven by a sense of purpose. They assess success not just in monetary terms but also in terms of their social influence.

Business Venturers

Corporate entrepreneurs are those who work for well-established companies yet nonetheless have entrepreneurial qualities and habits. They are internal innovators and change agents, or intrapreneurs. In order to increase the organization's competitive edge, corporate entrepreneurs are frequently entrusted with finding new development prospects, creating new goods or services, or streamlining current procedures.

In summary

The notion of entrepreneurship is broad and dynamic, including a variety of actions and ways of thinking. It is a way of thinking and seeing the world, not simply a simple economic venture. Individuals may release their ability to make a significant and long-lasting influence by adopting an entrepreneurial attitude and discovering their inner inventor. The traits of prosperous entrepreneurs, the process of cultivating an entrepreneurial attitude, and methods for overcoming typical obstacles faced by entrepreneurs will all be covered in the upcoming chapters.

Qualities of Profitable Business Owners

Entrepreneurs that are successful have a distinct set of traits that make them stand out from the competition. These qualities help them to lead innovation and achieve long-term success while navigating the difficulties and uncertainties of the commercial environment. This section will examine the essential traits of prosperous entrepreneurs and go over how you might develop these traits within yourself.

zeal and tenacity

Entrepreneurs that are successful do so because of their passion. They are prepared to go above and beyond to make their ideas a reality because they firmly and unwaveringly believe in them. Their enthusiasm not only spurs them on, but it also encourages others to follow in their footsteps. Entrepreneurs that are successful remain steadfast in the face of challenges and disappointments. They use failure as a chance to develop and learn because they recognize it as a necessary part of the process.

Creative Thought

Entrepreneurs that are successful have a visionary mentality. They possess the capacity to look beyond the here and now and imagine a future apart from the status quo. They don't hesitate to question received knowledge and are always looking for new and creative chances. Their ability to think creatively enables them to spot market gaps and create ground-breaking products that satisfy consumer demands.

Taking Chances and Being Strong

Being an entrepreneur is dangerous by nature, and successful businesspeople don't mind taking calculated chances. They are aware that there can be no benefit without risk. They are prepared to face uncertainty and leave their comfort zones behind. They do, yet, also have the resiliency to overcome obstacles and disappointments. Failures are seen as teaching opportunities, and they take use of them to hone their tactics and raise their chances of success.

Flexibility and Adaptability

Since the business environment is always changing, effective entrepreneurs have a flexible and adaptive attitude. They are willing to adjust their strategy in response to shifts in the market since they can detect them quickly. They are aware that obsolescence can result from rigidity and resistance to change. They remain ahead of the curve and have a competitive edge by welcoming change and adjusting to new situations.

Exceptional Leadership Capabilities

Entrepreneurs that are successful are born leaders. They possess the capacity to encourage and inspire others to share their vision and cooperate to achieve a common objective. They can successfully communicate their thoughts and expectations to their team since they have strong communication skills. They set an exemplary example for others to follow and don't mind getting their hands filthy. They may also assign assignments to their team members and encourage them to take responsibility for their work.

Originality & Creativity

The essence of entrepreneurship is in innovation, and those that are successful do it by nature. They are able to think creatively and unconventionally to solve challenging issues in novel ways. They don't hesitate to question the status quo and are always looking for fresh approaches to enhance already-existing goods or services. They inspire their team members to think creatively and cultivate an innovative culture inside their businesses.

Robust work ethic

Entrepreneurs that are successful have a strong work ethic and are prepared to invest the time and energy necessary to reach their objectives. They are aware that establishing a profitable business demands commitment and tenacity. They are prepared to put in long hours, make compromises, and put their jobs ahead of other responsibilities. They stand out from the crowd and do more tasks faster because to their strong work ethic.

Ongoing Education

Entrepreneurs that are successful have a voracious appetite for information and are dedicated to lifelong learning. They are aware that the business environment is ever-changing and that remaining informed is necessary to stay ahead of the curve. They study books, take part in networking events, go to industry conferences, and actively search for fresh knowledge. They are receptive to criticism and prepared to modify their plans in light of fresh discoveries and data.

Resilient Solvers of Problems

Obstacles and problems abound in entrepreneurship, and prosperous businesspeople are tough problem solvers. They possess the capacity to dissect difficult issues into digestible chunks and create workable answers. Setbacks don't stop them; instead, they see them as chances to improve and learn. They take a constructive approach to issues and are prepared to ask for assistance and guidance when required.

The intelligence of emotions

Entrepreneurs that are successful have excellent emotional intelligence. They are able to comprehend and control both their own and other people's emotions. They have the ability to forge close bonds with stakeholders, consumers, and other team members because they are compassionate. They can handle challenging topics with ease and are good communicators. Their capacity for emotional intelligence enables them to create a welcoming and encouraging work atmosphere.

In summary, prosperous businesspeople have a certain set of traits that allow them to succeed in the corporate world. You may develop a great business and unlock your inner innovator by developing these traits in yourself. Keep in mind that becoming an entrepreneur is a journey, and it takes time and work to acquire these qualities. Accept the difficulties, grow from your mistakes, and never give up on your vision.

Creating an Attitude of Entrepreneurship

To construct a profitable business and become a successful entrepreneur, you must cultivate an entrepreneurial attitude. This way of thinking is defined by a distinct combination of attitudes, convictions, and actions that help people spot opportunities, take measured risks, and overcome the difficulties of becoming an entrepreneur. Having an entrepreneurial attitude is essential not just for launching a company but also for maintaining long-term profitability and stimulating innovation.

Adopting a Growth Perspective

Adopting a growth mentality is one of the essential elements of an entrepreneurial attitude. This idea, made popular by psychologist Carol Dweck, contends that success is more likely to come to those who think they can improve their skills by effort, commitment, and education. On the other hand, those who have a fixed mindset think that they are limited in what they can do.

Entrepreneurs that embrace a growth mentality are more willing to take chances, learn from mistakes, and keep refining both their businesses and themselves. They regard obstacles as chances for development and consider failures to be priceless teaching moments. This kind of thinking raises an entrepreneur's chances of success by enabling them to overcome obstacles and learn from mistakes.

Developing an Intense Interest in Innovation

Cultivating an innovative enthusiasm is a crucial component in forming an entrepreneurial mentality. Entrepreneurs that are successful are motivated by a desire to invent new things, find solutions to challenges, and improve the world. They are always looking for new and creative ways to enhance the processes, goods, and services that already exist.

Entrepreneurs need to maintain their curiosity and open-mindedness in order to foster a love for innovation. They have to be on the lookout for novel concepts, fashions, and technological advancements that might upend established marketplaces or upend sectors. Entrepreneurs that remain up to date and pursue ongoing education are better able to spot market gaps and provide novel solutions that cater to consumers' wants and requirements.

Accepting Risk and Unpredictability

Since entrepreneurship is inherently dangerous, accepting risk and uncertainty is a necessary part of cultivating an entrepreneurial mindset. Growing and innovating requires taking measured risks, as successful businesspeople are aware of. They are prepared to take risks, go outside their comfort zones, and deal with the potential for failure.

But accepting risk does not equate to being careless. Entrepreneurs should carefully weigh the benefits and dangers of every choice they make, taking measured chances based on in-depth investigation and study. Additionally, they must to be ready to modify and refocus their plans in response to unforeseen difficulties or shifts in the marketplace.

Building Perseverance and Resilience

Resilience and persistence are necessary for creating a successful enterprise. Entrepreneurs frequently encounter many challenges and disappointments along the way; what makes them unique is their capacity to pick themselves up and carry on. Cultivating a never-give-up mentality and strengthening resilience are essential components of developing an entrepreneurial mindset.

Entrepreneurs that are resilient see setbacks as teaching moments and utilize them to improve their tactics and methods. They do not allow setbacks to impede their growth since they recognize that they are an inevitable part of the business path. Rather, they use what they've learned from their errors, modify their strategies, and keep working tirelessly to achieve their objectives.

Encouraging a proactive and results-driven approach

Proactive and focused on taking action, entrepreneurs possess an entrepreneurial attitude. They actively seek for and create chances rather than waiting for them to present themselves. They take the initiative, act swiftly, and don't hesitate to take the required actions to make their ideas a reality.

Setting specific objectives, creating workable plans, and carrying them out with vigor and commitment are all parts of a proactive and action-oriented approach. This type of entrepreneur doesn't hesitate to take the initial move, even if it means venturing into uncharted territory. They are prepared to make the sacrifices necessary to realize their goal because they recognize that progress can only be attained via action.

Creating a Support Network

Creating a support system is another aspect of cultivating an entrepreneurial attitude. Being an entrepreneur can be a lonely path, so having a solid support network may help you stay motivated, encouraged, and guided when things go tough. It may be quite beneficial to surround oneself with like-minded people, mentors, and advisers since they can offer insightful opinions, connections, and criticism.

It is recommended that entrepreneurs proactively pursue networking opportunities, become members of industry groups, and engage in entrepreneurial networks. Through establishing a network of support, entrepreneurs may have access to a multitude of information and assets, make connections with possible investors or partners, and locate mentors who can offer advice and encouragement all along their entrepreneurial path.

Accepting Lifelong Education

Lastly, a dedication to lifelong learning is necessary for cultivating an entrepreneurial attitude. Entrepreneurs that are successful recognize that the business environment is ever-changing and that they must always be learning and adapting to stay ahead of the curve. In order to improve their capacity for entrepreneurship, they actively seek out new information, experiences, and talents.

By participating in workshops, conferences, and seminars, reading books and articles about innovation and entrepreneurship, and looking for chances for professional growth, entrepreneurs may embrace lifelong learning. Entrepreneurs may constantly broaden their knowledge base and keep on top of industry trends and advances by maintaining an open mind and an inquisitive nature.

To sum up, cultivating an entrepreneurial attitude is crucial to being successful in the business world. Entrepreneurs can unleash their inner innovator and create a profitable business by adopting a growth mindset, igniting a passion for innovation, accepting risk and uncertainty, strengthening their resilience and perseverance, encouraging a proactive and action-oriented approach, creating a network of support, and embracing lifelong learning.

Overcoming Typical Obstacles in Entrepreneurship

It may be thrilling and fulfilling to launch a new business and adopt an entrepreneurial attitude. It is not without difficulties, though. In this part, we'll look at some typical challenges faced by business owners and talk about solutions.

Financial Limitations

Getting enough money for their projects is one of the biggest obstacles facing entrepreneurs. Inadequate financial resources might impede a company's expansion and progress. Entrepreneurs need to be imaginative and resourceful in their search for alternate funding sources if they are to overcome this obstacle.

Finding venture capitalists or angel investors who are prepared to invest in potential firms is one strategy. These investors can offer important contacts and experience in addition to financial help. Investigating government loans or grants intended to encourage entrepreneurial endeavors is an additional choice.

Entrepreneurs may also want to think about bootstrapping their companies, which entails funding operations using personal savings or money from early sales. This strategy necessitates cautious money management and a rush to income generation.

Insufficient Market Understanding

Any enterprise must comprehend its target market to be successful. Lack of market awareness, however, is a problem that many entrepreneurs have, particularly when they are targeting a niche market or breaking into a new sector.

Entrepreneurs should put time and effort into carrying out in-depth market research in order to overcome this obstacle.

This entails examining the requirements and preferences of customers, researching rivals, and spotting market trends. Entrepreneurs that have a thorough awareness of the market are better able to make judgments and create goods and services that satisfy consumer needs.

Entrepreneurs may also approach mentors or industry professionals with firsthand knowledge of the target market for advice. These people may offer insightful advice and support entrepreneurs in navigating the industry's complexity.

Fear of Not Getting Enough

One of the biggest problems that many entrepreneurs have is fear of failing. It may be quite debilitating to be afraid of taking chances and the likelihood that their endeavor would fail. But it's crucial to understand that failing is a normal part of becoming an entrepreneur and may teach you essential lessons for success in the future.

A growth mentality is what entrepreneurs need to get over their fear of failing. This entails accepting a willingness to take measured risks and seeing setbacks as teaching moments. Through redefining failure as a necessary step on the path to success, entrepreneurs may get over their worries and keep coming up with new ideas.

Surrounding oneself with a network of mentors, peers, and advisers who can offer support and direction during trying times is also beneficial for entrepreneurs. These people may provide insightful advice and support entrepreneurs in keeping an optimistic outlook.

Time Management: Entrepreneurs frequently have to juggle a lot of activities and obligations, which can result in ineffective time management. Sustaining productivity and ensuring that critical activities are prioritized need effective time management.

In order to overcome this obstacle, business owners need create a precise and practical timetable. This entails assigning time and establishing clear objectives and due dates for every assignment. Setting priorities for jobs according to their urgency and significance is crucial.

In order to optimize their workflow, entrepreneurs may also take use of productivity tools and technologies. Entrepreneurs may monitor their progress and maintain organization by using calendar tools, task management applications, and project management software.

Additionally, entrepreneurs may free up time to concentrate on high-value and strategic decision-making responsibilities by outsourcing specific operations or assigning jobs to dependable team members.

Putting Together a Powerful Team

One of the biggest challenges faced by entrepreneurs is assembling a cohesive and capable team. An enterprise's ability to succeed depends on its ability to hire people who fit its culture and have the requisite abilities.

Entrepreneurs should put time and effort into the hiring and selection process in order to overcome this obstacle. This entails outlining each team member's precise duties and responsibilities as well as the particular abilities and attributes needed.

When employing new team members, entrepreneurs should also give priority to cultural fit. A cohesive and cooperative workplace culture may stimulate creativity and propel the business forward. In addition to evaluating a candidate's technical proficiency, it's critical to evaluate their work ethic, morals, and teamwork abilities.

Additionally, business owners want to give their staff members continual opportunity for training and growth. This shows a dedication to their achievement and progress while also assisting in the improvement of their abilities and knowledge.

Handling Burnout and Stress

Being an entrepreneur can be a difficult and stressful job that frequently results in stress and burnout. It's critical for business owners to put self-care first and develop stress management techniques.

In order to overcome this obstacle, business owners should create a positive work-life balance. This entails establishing limits and scheduling time for rest, exercise, and private pursuits. Frequent physical activity, mindfulness exercises, and meditation can also help lower stress and enhance general wellbeing.

In order to receive emotional support and direction during trying times, entrepreneurs need also assemble a network of mentors, family members, and friends. Getting expert assistance, such as coaching or therapy, can also be helpful for stress management and mental health maintenance.

In conclusion, even if becoming an entrepreneur comes with its share of difficulties, these barriers may be surmounted with the appropriate attitude and techniques. Entrepreneurs may successfully navigate the entrepreneurial path and release their inner inventor to develop a successful company by resolving financial restrictions, improving market knowledge, embracing failure, managing time efficiently, assembling a strong team, and placing self-care first.

Locating Innovation
Possibilities
Identifying Needs and Gaps in the Market

Having a thorough grasp of the market you are entering is essential for success as an inventor and entrepreneur. This entails figuring out the gaps and demands in the market as well as chances for innovation. By doing this, you may provide goods and services that satisfy customer needs and provide your business a competitive edge.

Recognizing Market Divides

Market gaps are places in a market where there aren't enough goods or services to satisfy customers' wants. These gaps may occur for a number of reasons, including evolving technology, shifting consumer preferences, or deficiencies in current offers. Finding chances for innovation and creating solutions that fill in these gaps in the market requires an understanding of these gaps.

Entrepreneurs need to perform in-depth market research and analysis in order to pinpoint holes in the market. To do this, research the target market, comprehend customer behavior, and pinpoint any pain areas or unmet demands. Entrepreneurs can clearly see the gaps in the market and the possible prospects for innovation by obtaining data and insights.

Determining the Needs of the Market

Entrepreneurs need to recognize market requirements as well as holes in the market. Market needs are the unique demands and preferences of customers within a certain market. Through comprehension of these demands, business owners may create goods and services that satisfy them, adding value for clients and propelling their endeavors to accomplishment.

A thorough grasp of the target market's demographics, tastes, and habits is necessary to identify market demands. Through focus groups, questionnaires, market research, and other data collecting techniques, entrepreneurs may obtain this information. Entrepreneurs may obtain significant insights into market demands and create creative solutions by listening to their customers and understanding their goals and pain areas.

Analysis and Research on the Market

Finding gaps and demands in the market requires a thorough understanding of market research and analysis. This include obtaining and examining information on the competition, the target market, and market trends. Entrepreneurs may obtain important insights that guide their innovation initiatives and assist them in making well-informed company decisions by carrying out thorough market research.

Primary and secondary data collection is a part of market research. Information obtained directly from the target market through surveys, interviews, or observations is referred to as primary data. Conversely, secondary data pertains to pre-existing information that has been gathered from many sources, including government publications, market research studies, and industry reports. Through the integration of primary and secondary data, business owners may obtain a comprehensive comprehension of the industry and recognize opportunities for innovation.

Analyzing the gathered data to find opportunities, trends, and patterns is known as market analysis. Analyzing customer behavior, market size, development potential, the competitive environment, and other pertinent variables are all part of this. Entrepreneurs may find holes in the market, comprehend customer wants, and create novel products that address those needs by performing a thorough market study.

Client Testimonials and Verification

It takes more than just market research and analysis to identify gaps and demands in the market; customer input and opportunity validation are also important steps in this process. Feedback from customers is quite helpful in figuring out their preferences, problems, and wants. Entrepreneurs may obtain valuable insights that aid in honing their concepts and creating inventive solutions that genuinely satisfy clients by interacting with them and soliciting their input.

The practice of examining and verifying the level of market demand for a good or service is called customer validation. This entails developing MVPs, or minimum viable products, and getting input from prospective clients. Before completely launching their companies, entrepreneurs may confirm the market demand for their inventions and make required revisions by putting their ideas to the test in the market and getting feedback.

Comparative Evaluation

Entrepreneurs must not only comprehend the gaps and wants in the industry, but also carry out a competition study to pinpoint current market participants and assess their products. This include researching the goods, prices, promotions, and general market positioning of rival companies. Through competitive analysis, entrepreneurs may spot areas for distinction and create novel products that provide clients with something special.

Through competitive analysis, business owners may learn about the advantages and disadvantages of their rivals and pinpoint areas in which they might excel. Entrepreneurs may establish a competitive edge and position their companies for success by providing a distinctive value proposition and meeting unmet client demands.

Keeping Up with Market Developments

It's also necessary to remain ahead of market trends and disruptions in order to identify gaps and demands. Both markets and consumer tastes are dynamic. They are always changing. Entrepreneurs who monitor market trends are able to spot new possibilities and provide creative solutions that meet changing client demands.

In order to stay ahead of market trends, one must keep an eye on trade fairs and conferences, interact with thought leaders and subject matter experts, and watch industry news. Entrepreneurs may proactively discover market gaps and demands and position their businesses as industry leaders by keeping up to date with the latest developments and trends.

To sum up, one of the most important phases in the innovation process is identifying market gaps and demands. Through discerning unfulfilled client demands and pinpointing market gaps, entrepreneurs may devise inventive solutions that provide value and propel their businesses to success. Entrepreneurs may find possibilities for innovation and establish a solid basis for their businesses by performing competitive analysis, obtaining consumer feedback, doing

in-depth market research and analysis, and staying ahead of
industry trends.

Disruptions and Trends

Innovation is more than simply creating original ideas; it also involves spotting market trends and upheavals. Entrepreneurs are able to position themselves to take advantage of new chances and remain ahead of the competition by knowing the present market and projecting future changes. This section will examine the role that trends and disruptions play in fostering innovation and the ways in which business owners may take advantage of them to launch profitable endeavors.

The Influence of Patterns

Patterns or changes in the market that have a big influence on consumer behavior and industry sectors are called trends. They may result from a number of things, including developments in technology, adjustments in consumer tastes, changes in the economy, or social and cultural movements. Entrepreneurs must be aware of and comprehend these trends since they offer important insights into new business prospects and possible market gaps.

Recognizing trends may help you predict and address client requirements before they become popular, which is one of the primary advantages. Entrepreneurs may establish themselves as leaders in their sector and obtain a competitive edge by staying ahead of the curve. For instance, many prosperous businesspeople saw the rise of e-commerce and internet purchasing early on. Companies like Amazon and Alibaba transformed the retail sector and rose to prominence by using this tendency.

Entrepreneurs must be aware and continuously observe the market in order to spot trends. Market research, industry conferences and events, following thought leaders and influencers in the field, data analysis, and consumer insights are some ways to do this. Through vigilant monitoring of the market, entrepreneurs are able to identify new trends and modify their approaches accordingly.

Accepting Interruptions

Contrarily, disruptions are notable adjustments or inventions that upend established markets or corporate structures. They have the power to totally alter how goods and services are provided, used, and enjoyed. Technological developments, alterations in regulations, or changes in consumer behavior can all cause disruptions.

Disruptions provide enormous potential for entrepreneurs even if they might be perceived as dangers to well-established enterprises. Entrepreneurs may generate inventive solutions that tackle novel market demands and obstacles by welcoming disruptions and modifying their company models accordingly. For instance, the emergence of ride-sharing services such as Uber and Lyft upended the conventional taxi sector by providing a more practical and cost-effective substitute.

Entrepreneurs that want to take advantage of disruptions must be flexible and prepared to question the status quo. They should aggressively look for chances to upend established markets or sectors. It takes an inquisitive, flexible, and risk-taking attitude to do this. Entrepreneurs have the opportunity to take the lead and mold the future of their businesses by embracing disruptions.

The Function of Technology

Both trends and disruptions are mostly driven by technology. Technological developments have the ability to change markets, industries, and our way of living and working. Entrepreneurs are better able to see chances for innovation when they comprehend the possibilities of technology and how it affects their respective sectors.

Artificial intelligence, blockchain, the Internet of Things (IoT), and virtual reality are some of the technological innovations that are changing a number of industries, including healthcare, banking, retail, and entertainment. By keeping up with these trends, entrepreneurs may use them to develop cutting-edge goods, services, and business strategies.

Additionally, entrepreneurs now find it simpler to recognize and react to trends and disruptions because to technology. Entrepreneurs may learn a great deal about market trends, competitive environments, and customer behavior by utilizing the wealth of data and analytics technologies at their disposal. With this data-driven approach, entrepreneurs can create strategies that meet market expectations and make well-informed decisions.

Adjusting to Shifting Consumer Attitudes

Determining trends and disruptions requires an understanding of customer behavior. Business owners must modify their tactics to satisfy shifting customer preferences. Entrepreneurs who remain aware of the demands and preferences of their target market are able to spot new trends and provide creative solutions that appeal to them.

For instance, the increasing popularity of environmentally conscious and sustainable products has given rise to businesses that place a high priority on environmental stewardship. Early adopters of this movement saw opportunities to build profitable businesses that appeal to ethical consumers.

Entrepreneurs should spend money on consumer insights and market research in order to adjust to shifting consumer behavior. They have to actively interact, solicit input, and pay attention to the wants and needs of their target market. Strong customer connections may provide entrepreneurs with insightful information that spurs innovation and keeps them one step ahead of the competition.

Working together and establishing connections

Innovation frequently involves teamwork. Through networking and engaging with thought leaders, industry experts, and other entrepreneurs, business owners may obtain important insights and fresh ideas and views. Effectively navigating upheavals and capitalizing on trends may be facilitated by collaborative partnerships for entrepreneurs.

Taking part in networking events, joining professional groups, and attending industry conferences are all excellent methods to meet like-minded people and create a solid support system. Entrepreneurs may access a multitude of information and experience by surrounding themselves with a broad set of people, which can support their efforts in innovation.

To sum up, trends and disruptions are important forces behind innovation. Entrepreneurs may see new possibilities and launch profitable businesses by identifying and comprehending these market trends. Effectively harnessing trends and disruptions requires being educated, accepting change, utilizing technology, adjusting to customer behavior, and working with others. By doing this, business owners may unlock their creative potential and create successful enterprises in a world that is changing quickly.

Originality and Idea Generation

Innovation is fueled by creativity. It is the capacity to think creatively, to generate original ideas, and to recognize possibilities where others perceive barriers. When it comes to entrepreneurship, creativity plays a crucial role in recognizing and creating novel concepts that have the potential to become profitable businesses.

Innovation's Crucial Role in Entrepreneurship

Many people believe that creativity is what propels entrepreneurship. It is what distinguishes business owners from the general public. Though many individuals may have brilliant ideas, what sets entrepreneurs apart is their capacity to make those ideas a reality. Entrepreneurs with creativity are able to spot opportunities where others perceive barriers and devise original solutions to issues.

Creativity in the context of enterprise extends beyond aesthetics and design. It includes a wider variety of competencies, such as critical thinking, problem-solving, and the capacity to make connections between seemingly unrelated ideas. It involves questioning the existing quo and adopting new perspectives.

Developing Originality

Being creative is not something that just a few people possess. It's a talent that may be cultivated and enhanced with time. The following are some methods to foster creativity:

Accept Curiosity

The spark that ignites creativity is curiosity. It is the drive to investigate, discover, and comprehend the environment we live in. Entrepreneurs may expose themselves to novel experiences, concepts, and viewpoints by embracing curiosity. They are able to challenge presumptions, pose queries, and look for fresh information. Entrepreneurs with curiosity are able to identify connections and patterns that others might miss, which inspires creative thinking.

Encourage an Imaginative Environment

Idea generation requires the establishment of a creatively supportive atmosphere. This involves creating an environment that promotes experimentation, cooperation, and open communication. It entails fostering an environment where people feel free to express their ideas and take chances, and where innovation is valued and rewarded. Entrepreneurs may encourage their team members to think creatively and participate in the innovation process by creating a creative atmosphere.

Engage in Divergent Thinking

The capacity to come up with several ideas and solutions for a situation is known as divergent thinking. It entails letting go of preconceived notions and considering alternative options. Entrepreneurs may use mind mapping, brainstorming sessions, and other creative exercises that promote the production of a wide variety of ideas to practice divergent thinking. Divergent thinking may help entrepreneurs find original and creative ideas.

Accept Failure and Gain Knowledge from Errors

An essential component of becoming an entrepreneur is failure. However, entrepreneurs should welcome failure as a chance for personal development and education rather than seeing it as a setback. Entrepreneurs may get over their fear of failing and take more chances by redefining failure as a necessary step on the path to success. Entrepreneurs are able to build upon their initial notions, polish their ideas, and iterate by learning from their failures.

Methods for Generating Ideas

Coming up with creative ideas needs a methodical approach. Entrepreneurs might employ the following strategies to encourage the production of ideas:

generating ideas

One well-liked method for coming up with ideas in a group situation is brainstorming. It entails bringing together a varied group of people and empowering them to openly and judgment-free exchange opinions. Regardless matter how feasible or useful an idea is, the aim is to produce a lot of them. Through mutual innovation and idea sharing, entrepreneurs may find novel and creative solutions.

Mental Maps

An effective visual tool for entrepreneurs to arrange their ideas and thoughts is mind mapping. It entails centering a visual depiction of the primary topic or issue on a page, then spreading out with notions and ideas that are linked. Mind mapping fosters creativity and makes links between disparate ideas visible to business owners.

SCAMPER Method

The SCAMPER method is a methodical way to generate ideas. It entails posing a sequence of queries to encourage original thought. In SCAMPER, every letter stands for a distinct question:

Replace: What may be changed or replaced?

What is it possible to merge or combine?

Adapt: How may the concept be changed or adjusted?

Change: How may the concept be adjusted or changed?

Repurposed: What additional uses may there be for the concept?

Eliminate: What may be taken out or done away with?

Reverse: In what ways may the concept be turned or inverted?

Through a methodical application of these inquiries to an established concept or issue, entrepreneurs might provide novel and inventive resolutions.

USING TECHNOLOGY TO Generate Ideas

Technology has completely changed how business owners come up with and refine their ideas. The following are some methods for using technology to generate ideas:

Internet Idea Platforms

Entrepreneurs may exchange and work together on ideas on online idea platforms. Through these platforms, people with various specialties and backgrounds may interact and share their own viewpoints. Through the utilization of crowdsourcing, entrepreneurs may access an extensive repository of concepts and perceptions.

Information Analysis

Trends and insightful information from data analytics can inspire creative thinking. Through the examination of extensive data sets, business owners may see trends, weaknesses, and openings in the industry. Entrepreneurs may generate creative ideas and make well-informed decisions with the aid of this data-driven method to idea development.

Social Media Monitoring

Social networking sites offer a multitude of data on the needs, tastes, and trends of its users. Through attentively listening to discussions and keeping an eye on social media platforms, business owners may obtain important knowledge about what their target audience is interested in. With this data, creative solutions and concepts that fill gaps in the market may be produced.

To sum up, the entrepreneurial mindset is reliant on innovation and idea development. Through idea creation techniques, divergent thinking, and creativity cultivation, entrepreneurs may unleash their creative potential and generate novel concepts. Technology can be quite helpful in generating ideas as well, giving business owners access to a multitude of concepts and perspectives. Through the embrace of creativity and the utilization of technology, entrepreneurs may unleash their creative potential and establish prosperous businesses.

Assessing and Choosing Creative Concepts

The following stage is to assess and choose the most promising ideas for additional development once you have produced a pool of original and inventive concepts. Making sure that the ideas you put your time, money, and effort into have the best chance of succeeding is what this process is all about. This section will examine several approaches and standards for assessing and choosing creative concepts.

Standards for Assessment

Establishing a set of standards for creative idea evaluation that are in line with your overarching business goals and objectives is crucial. These standards will function as a foundation for evaluating each idea's viability and potential. Here are a few typical standards to take into account:

Market Potential: Evaluate the target market's size and the level of demand for the suggested remedy. Does the concept address a noteworthy need or issue? Will the concept bring in money and add value for clients?

Competitive Advantage: Assess the idea's originality and distinctiveness. Does it provide a competitive edge over already-available market solutions? Does it have a distinct value proposition that makes it stand out from rivals?

Technical, operational, and financial viability of the concept should all be taken into account. Can it be carried out given the limitations and resources at hand? Exist any logistical or technological obstacles that need to be addressed?

Scalability: Evaluate the idea's ability to expand and scale. Is it possible to broaden its scope to cater to a more diverse range of sectors or geographical areas? Is there potential for innovation and growth in the future?

Alignment with Core Values: Assess the degree to which the proposal complies with the goals, mission, and core values of your business. Does it align with your overarching strategic plan? Will it help your business be successful and sustainable in the long run?

Methods of Evaluation

Innovative concept comparison and evaluation may be accomplished with a variety of techniques and resources. Here are a few popular strategies:

Perform a SWOT analysis on every concept to identify its advantages, disadvantages, opportunities, and threats. This study aids in determining the concept's advantages and disadvantages from inside as well as potential external opportunities and market threats.

Analyze the possible costs and advantages of each concept using the cost-benefit method. Think about the amount of money needed, the possible return on investment, and the idea's overall profitability.

Testing using prototypes: Create minimal viable products (MVPs) or prototypes to test and get feedback on the idea's viability and attractiveness. This enables you to verify presumptions, spot possible enhancements, and make defensible choices depending on user input.

Expert Evaluation: Consult mentors, advisers, or industry professionals who have experience in your sector for advice and comments. Their knowledge and experience might offer insightful viewpoints and assist you in reaching better conclusions.

Customer validation: Talk to prospective clients to get their opinions and confirm if there is a market for the concept.

To find out about their requirements, preferences, and readiness to pay for the suggested solution, do focus groups, surveys, or interviews.

Process of Making Decisions

It's time to decide which of the creative ideas to follow further after you have compared and assessed them using the previously described standards and techniques. The following steps will help you make decisions:

Prioritize and rank: Give each concept a score or rating according to the assessment criteria. This will assist you in ranking the concepts and concentrating on those that have the most promise.

Think About Resource Allocation: Assess the assets, skills, and potential of your project. Think about the resources—money, time, and experience—needed to create and execute each project. Select concepts that make sense given the resources at your disposal and that you can really carry out.

Involve important stakeholders, team members, or advisers in the decision-making process in order to reach a consensus. To guarantee a comprehensive assessment and secure support for the chosen concepts, solicit their opinions and insights.

Test and Repeat: Keep in mind that this is a continuous process of evaluation. Continue testing, iterating, and improving the concepts you've chosen as you proceed, taking into account market conditions and real-world input.

Learn from Failure: Accept that it's possible to fail and see it as a chance to grow. It's OK that not every concept will be implemented. In future decision-making and innovation endeavors, apply the knowledge gained from failed ideas.

You may raise your chances of finding and developing creative ideas that could propel your business's success by adhering to a methodical examination and selection procedure. As you traverse the ever-changing terrain of innovation, never forget to stay flexible, open-minded, and eager to take measured chances.

Building a Strong
Foundation for Your Venture

You may raise your chances of finding and developing creative ideas that could propel your business's success by adhering to a methodical examination and selection procedure. As you traverse the ever-changing terrain of innovation, never forget to stay flexible, open-minded, and eager to take measured chances.

Clarifying Your Goals

Your vision is the ultimate objective or destination you wish to reach with your business. It ought to be aspirational, motivating, and consistent with your beliefs and values. Think about the following inquiries as you define your vision:

What kind of global influence do you hope your project will have?

What need or issue are you attempting to address?

What impact do you hope your initiative will have?

Your goal should be clear and precise at the same time as being flexible and adaptable to your venture's changing needs. It should also be conveyed in a style that appeals to your group, stakeholders, and possible clients.

Formulating Your Objective

Your mission statement outlines the objectives and actions of your endeavor, whereas your vision statement sets the overall direction. "What do we do and why do we do it?" is addressed. Take into account the following components when creating your mission:

Which goods and services do you provide?

Who are the clients you hope to attract?

What distinguishes your business from rivals?

What principles and beliefs guide your decision-making process?

Make sure your mission statement is clear, succinct, and focused on taking action. It should convey the advantages your business offers to stakeholders and consumers and showcase its distinctive value proposition.

Vision and Mission Alignment

It is essential that your vision and mission are in sync for your endeavor to succeed. Your vision should be clearly reflected in your mission statement, which will include the precise tactics and plans you will use to get to your ideal future state. While coordinating your vision and objective, take into account the following:

Make sure your vision is supported by and helps to realize your objective.

To make sure your purpose is still pertinent and in line with your changing objectives, review it frequently.

To establish a feeling of purpose and direction among your team, stakeholders, and clients, clearly communicate your vision and goal.

Your business will have a solid foundation and a clear path to success if your vision and purpose are in line.

Sharing Your Mission and Vision

It is crucial to convey your vision and goal to your staff, stakeholders, and consumers once you have established them. A common understanding and dedication to the objectives of your endeavor may be developed by regular and clear communication of your vision and purpose.

The following techniques can help you convey your vision and goal effectively:

Internal Communication: Make sure your team members comprehend and support your vision and purpose by sharing it with them. To keep everyone engaged and in sync, provide updates and developments on the vision and mission on a regular basis.

External Communication: Make sure all of your stakeholders, like as partners, consumers, and investors, understand your vision and objective. Communicate your mission and beliefs using a variety of platforms, including your website, social media accounts, and promotional materials.

Storytelling: To make your vision and purpose a reality, employ storytelling tactics. Tell tales and provide instances of how your project is changing the world and achieving its goals. This encourages others to support your endeavor and helps to establish an emotional connection.

Visual Representation: To help people remember and understand your vision and goal, put it in the form of infographics or diagrams. Images can make difficult concepts understandable and interesting.

Consistency: Make sure that all of the platforms and interactions you use to communicate your vision and mission are consistent. Being consistent strengthens the identity and purpose of your enterprise and fosters trust.

Recall that communicating your vision and goal effectively is a continuous effort. Make sure your messaging is still current and appealing to your stakeholders by reviewing and improving it on a regular basis.

Motivating and Inspiring Others

In addition to giving your business direction, a strong vision and mission statement encourage and inspire people to join you on your path. People are more inclined to support your endeavor and help it succeed if they are moved by your vision and goal.

Here are some ideas for motivating and inspiring people:

Set a good example for others by acting and making choices that reflect your dedication to your vision and goal. Set an example for your team and other stakeholders by living and breathing the mission of your business.

Tell Success Stories: To demonstrate the strides you are making toward realizing your goal, highlight the successes and effects of your endeavor. In order to motivate others and foster a sense of pride and achievement, celebrate achievements and tell success stories.

Empower and Involve Others: Provide your stakeholders and team members with the chance to help you realize your goal and vision. Encourage their opinions and suggestions and provide them the freedom to assume responsibility for their jobs.

Acknowledge and Appreciate: Give credit where credit is due for the efforts and contributions of people and groups that share your vision and goals. Acknowledge their accomplishments and offer rewards that reaffirm the significance of the goal of your endeavor.

People who are inspired and motivated by you build a community that is engaged and supportive of your endeavor, which increases the chances of long-term success.

A crucial first step in developing a profitable business is coming up with an engaging vision and purpose. Your mission statement describes the goals and actions of your endeavor, but your vision statement sets the ultimate course and aim.

You create a solid basis for your venture's success by ensuring that your vision and goal are in sync, expressing them clearly, and motivating people. Keep in mind that having a captivating vision and mission statement will not only direct your actions but also encourage and inspire people to join you on your path.

Developing
a Solid Business Plan

Successful businesses are based on a strong foundation, which is a well-crafted business strategy. It acts as a roadmap, assisting company owners in making well-informed decisions as they proceed through the several phases of their venture. Careful consideration, investigation, and analysis are necessary while creating a business strategy in order to make sure that every facet of the endeavor is taken into account. This section will examine the essential elements of a strong business plan and offer suggestions for creating one that will position your company for success.

Executive Synopsis

Your company plan is succinctly summarized in the executive summary. It should give a succinct and engaging overview of your business, emphasizing its special selling point and chances for success. Readers should be drawn in by this part and encouraged to learn more about your proposal. A succinct synopsis of your company, your target market, your competitive edge, and your financial predictions should all be included.

Description of the Company

The part on company description gives a thorough rundown of your business. It need to contain details about your company's goals and objectives, your goods and services, and your business's characteristics. Additionally, your USP should be highlighted in this part along with an explanation of how your business differs from the competitors. It's also crucial to provide information regarding your company's legal structure, such as whether it's a corporation, partnership, or sole proprietorship.

Analysis of the Market

To comprehend the business environment and spot development prospects, a comprehensive market study is essential. An evaluation of your target market's size, composition, and purchase patterns should be included in this section. Along with identifying the main rivals and their advantages and disadvantages, it should also assess the competitive environment. Moreover, identifying possible obstacles and creating plans to overcome them may be facilitated by performing a SWOT (Strengths, Weaknesses, Opportunities, and Threats) analysis.

Line of Products or Services

You should give a thorough explanation of your goods or services in this area. Describe how they satisfy the demands of your intended audience and emphasize the special qualities and advantages they offer. It's critical to state your offers' value proposition in straightforward terms and provide evidence for why buyers should pick your goods or services over those of your rivals. You should also provide a roadmap for product development and any future growth or diversification goals.

Sales & Marketing Plan

To draw in and keep consumers, a clear marketing and sales plan is necessary. Your target market should be described in this part, along with your strategy for reaching and interacting with them. It should include information about your distribution routes, price policy, and marketing initiatives. A sales forecast that details your anticipated revenue and sales goals should also be included.

Management and Operations

An outline of the organization and administration of your project may be found in the operations and management section. It need to contain details on your main players, their roles and duties, and your organizational structure. You should also provide an overview of your operating procedures, such as quality assurance, logistics, and manufacturing. It's critical to show that you have a well-thought-out plan in place for successfully and efficiently providing clients with your goods or services.

Budgetary Estimates

Projections for finances are an essential part of every company plan. They offer an estimate of the total income, total costs, and total profitability of your business. A thorough income statement, balance sheet, and cash flow statement should all be included in this part. It is crucial that you clearly explain how you arrived at your estimates and that your forecasts are based on reasonable assumptions. A break-even analysis and a summary of your financial needs should also be included.

Examination of Risks

Every endeavor has some risk, which you should recognize and try to reduce. You should perform a detailed risk analysis in this area, identifying possible dangers and providing ways to reduce their impact. Risks associated with competitive markets, shifting laws and regulations, and tight budgets may all fall under this category. You will inspire trust in potential investors and stakeholders by proving that you have thought through possible risks and have measures in place to address them.

Implementation Schedule

Your business plan's implementation strategy describes the actions you'll take to make it a reality. Together with a thorough action plan for every step of the project, it should also include a timetable with important deliverables and milestones. Any resource needs, including those for staff, machinery, or technology, should be covered in this area as well. You may show that you have considered the practical concerns of carrying out your business strategy by offering a detailed and well-organized implementation plan.

Creating a strong business plan is a crucial first step in creating a profitable endeavor. A thorough consideration, investigation, and evaluation are necessary to guarantee that every facet of your endeavor is taken into account. You will be well-equipped to create a business plan that positions your endeavor for success if you adhere to the rules described in this section. Recall that a strong business plan serves as both a blueprint and an effective instrument for obtaining capital, recruiting investors, and directing your decision-making.

Comprehending Market Research and Analysis

Doing market research and analysis is crucial to creating a solid basis for your business. Understanding the market and its dynamics can help you create plans and make well-informed decisions that will provide your company a competitive advantage. We will discuss the value of market research and analysis in this part, along with the essential procedures for carrying out efficient research.

The Value of Market Analysis

The process of obtaining and examining data on the target market, clients, rivals, and market trends is known as market research. It offers insightful information that may assist you in seeing chances, comprehending client wants, and coming to wise company selections. For your business, market research is essential for the following main reasons:

Finding the Needs and Preferences of the Customer

You may obtain a thorough grasp of your target market's requirements, preferences, and pain areas by conducting market research. You may get useful input to help you customize your goods or services to match consumer needs by holding focus groups, interviews, and surveys. Gaining an understanding of your consumers' preferences can help you stand out from the competition and create a special value offer.

Evaluating the Potential and Size of the Market

Your target market's size and potential may be ascertained with the use of market research. You may determine the total market demand for your product or service as well as the number of potential clients by examining industry reports, market trends, and demographic data. For the purpose of estimating revenue, creating reasonable sales goals, and making well-informed decisions on market entrance and expansion, this data is essential.

Assessing Rivals

By conducting market research, you may evaluate the advantages, disadvantages, and positioning of your rivals. You can find market gaps that your business can address by examining their offerings, pricing policies, promotional plans, and client feedback. Knowing what your rivals are giving can also help you set yourself apart from the competition and create a special value proposition that appeals to your target market.

Recognizing Opportunities and Trends in the Market

You may keep informed about upcoming prospects, technical breakthroughs, and industry trends by conducting market research. New markets, unexplored niches, and possible opportunities for innovation may all be found by keeping an eye on consumer behavior and market shifts. With the help of this knowledge, you will be able to modify your company plan and take advantage of chances before your rivals.

Procedures for Carrying Out Market Research

Several essential steps are part of a systematic method that is necessary to conduct efficient market research. The following are the crucial actions you should do while gathering market research for your business:

Establish Your Research Goals

Clearly defining your study objectives is essential before you begin. What particular details are you looking for? Which research questions do you have? Setting goals will keep you on task and guarantee that you collect the necessary information to support your decisions.

Choose Your Research Approach

Selecting the best research approach is necessary once you have established your study objectives. You can employ a number of techniques, such as focus groups, surveys, interviews, observation, and secondary data analysis. Select the approach that best fits your study goals and available resources from among the available methods, as each has pros and cons.

Gather Information

Gathering the information required to respond to your research questions is the next stage. You will need to create and distribute surveys, hold focus groups or interviews, or watch how customers behave if you are doing primary research. In the event that secondary data is being used, you will obtain information from already-published sources including government publications, trade journals, and internet databases.

Evaluate and Comprehend Information

It's time to examine and evaluate the data after you've gathered it. To do this, the data must be arranged, patterns and trends must be found, and insightful conclusions must be made. Large dataset analysis might benefit from the use of statistical analysis techniques and software to spot correlations or patterns that might not be obvious at first look.

Draw Inferences and Offer Suggestions

You are able to derive findings and offer well-informed suggestions for your endeavor based on the examination of your facts. These suggestions might involve altering your target market segmentation, pricing plans, marketing techniques, or supply of goods or services. It's critical that your recommendations be supported by substantial data and that they complement your overarching company goals.

Keep an eye on and update

Conducting market research is a constant activity, and it's critical to keep an eye on and update your research results. Rapid changes in markets and consumer tastes make it imperative to keep abreast of industry trends, rivalry, and customer input. As your business develops, you can remain ahead of the curve and make wise decisions by routinely analyzing and updating your market research.

Issues and Things to Think About in Market Research

Market research has many benefits for your business, but there are also drawbacks and things to think about. The following are typical obstacles that you could run into when performing market research:

Limited Assets

Doing market research may be expensive and time-consuming, particularly for small and fledgling companies with little funding. It's crucial to pick the most significant research goals and manage your resources carefully. To obtain the required data within your budget, think about utilizing affordable research techniques like online surveys or secondary data analysis.

Sample Size and Bias

Your research's validity and reliability may be impacted by bias and sample size. Making ensuring your data gathering techniques are impartial and your research sample is reflective of your target market is crucial. To reduce bias and boost the dependability of your findings, think about employing random sampling strategies and verifying your conclusions using a variety of data sources or research procedures.

Shifting Market Structures

Because markets are dynamic and ever-changing, conducting market research may be difficult. Rapid changes in consumer tastes, industry trends, and competitive landscapes need staying current and modifying your research strategy as necessary. You can remain on top of trends and make wise judgments by keeping a close eye on customer behavior and market developments.

Moral Aspects to Take into Account

The process of doing market research include gathering and evaluating data from people or businesses. It is crucial to make sure that your data gathering procedures and research methodologies abide by ethical standards and laws. Get participants' informed consent, respect their privacy and confidentiality, and only utilize the information gathered for study.

Doing market research and analysis is essential to creating a solid basis for your business. Understanding your target market, clients, rivals, and market trends can help you create plans and make well-informed decisions that will spur success and innovation. Don't forget to specify your research goals, pick a suitable technique, gather and evaluate data, make conclusions, and keep an eye on and update your research findings on a regular basis. Market research is an effective instrument that will enable you to unlock your inner creative and create a successful business, despite the difficulties.

Creating a Powerful Team

Any enterprise must have a solid team in order to succeed. If you're an entrepreneur with a great concept and an engaging vision, your business could not succeed if you don't have the necessary team to carry it out. In this section, we will discuss the value of forming a solid team and offer doable tactics for putting together a group of bright people who can assist in realizing your creative concepts.

Specifying Duties and Positions

Determining the duties and responsibilities of each team member is one of the first stages towards creating an effective team. To make sure that everyone is on the same page and working towards the same objective, it will be helpful to clearly outline the tasks and expectations for each job. When establishing positions, take into account the particular knowledge and abilities needed for each position and look for people who fit the bill.

Creating a distinct hierarchy within the team is also crucial. Having a chosen leader who can make final choices and offer direction can assist speed the decision-making process and reduce disagreements, even though teamwork and open communication are essential.

Selecting the Correct Personnel

It might be difficult to find the perfect people for your team. Searching for people that not only fit your venture's beliefs and culture but also possess the requisite expertise and abilities is crucial. When hiring, take into account using in-depth tests and interviews to gauge a candidate's aptitude and compatibility with the company.

Another crucial element to take into account when assembling a powerful team is diversity. You can create an atmosphere that is more creative and imaginative by bringing people together who have varied backgrounds, viewpoints, and areas of expertise. A varied staff can provide fresh perspectives and methods for handling problems, producing more substantial and fruitful results.

Promoting Cooperation and Interaction

A strong team must have effective communication and teamwork. Encourage team members to communicate honestly and openly with one another, fostering an atmosphere where people feel free to voice their opinions, worries, and suggestions. Frequent brainstorming sessions and team meetings may promote cooperation and guarantee that everyone is pursuing the same goals.

In the digital world we live in today, using technological tools and platforms may help improve communication and teamwork. Even if team members are spread out geographically, they may stay connected and simplify communication with the use of video conferencing tools, instant messaging applications, and project management software.

Offering Opportunities for Training and Development

For both the success of your business and the growth of your staff, it is imperative that you invest in their training and development. Whether via online courses, seminars, or workshops, offer options for ongoing education. Motivate team members to increase their expertise in fields that are pertinent to their positions and the project's overarching objectives.

Think about starting mentorship programs inside your staff as well. Putting seasoned team members in pairs with inexperienced or less seasoned ones might promote information exchange and career advancement. Team members can develop more quickly with the aid of mentors who can offer direction, encouragement, and insightful advice based on their personal experiences.

Creating a Culture of Hope and Support

Building a strong and cohesive team requires cultivating a pleasant and encouraging culture inside the group. Promote a climate of mutual respect, trust, and cooperation so that team members have a sense of worth and encouragement. Acknowledge and celebrate both individual and group accomplishments to inspire drive and pride.

Encourage a healthy work-life balance and give your team members' wellbeing first priority. Promote vacations, getaways, and time spent on personal interests. A team that is in good health and balance is more likely to be innovative, resilient, and productive when faced with obstacles.

Handling Disagreement and Finding Solutions

There will always be conflict in a team environment. It's critical for leaders to resolve disputes amicably and quickly. When disagreements emerge, promote candid communication and attentive listening to give team members a chance to voice their worries and points of view. Investigate the underlying reasons of disputes and try to come up with win-win solutions.

If disputes don't go away or get worse, you might want to think about bringing in an impartial third party, such a mediator, to aid with settlement. Finding a solution that is just and acceptable to all parties concerned should always be the aim, along with keeping the venture's best interests in mind.

Encouraging and Assigning

It might be alluring for an entrepreneur to attempt to handle everything themselves. Nonetheless, empowering and delegating are necessary for creating a good team. Give your team members the freedom to decide for themselves and to use their special talents and knowledge. Have faith in them to take responsibility for their jobs and obligations.

Delegating effectively entails setting clear expectations, giving team members the tools and assistance they need, and giving them the freedom to do their work independently. In addition to reducing your own burden, team empowerment encourages a sense of accountability and ownership among participants.

Assessing and Acknowledging Performance

It's critical to routinely assess your team members' work in order to pinpoint areas for development and acknowledge exceptional accomplishments. To support people's development, clearly define performance metrics and offer helpful criticism. Acknowledge and honor outstanding work, either with cash rewards, job advancements, or public acknowledgement.

It's also critical to deal with poor performance as soon as possible in a positive way. supply tools and support to team members so they may grow, and if more coaching or training is required, supply it. Creating a high-performing team that is driven, involved, and dedicated to the project's success should be the ultimate objective.

Developing a good team is an ongoing process that calls for constant attention and effort. You may lay the groundwork for success and realize the full potential of your creative ideas by devoting time and money to putting together a skilled and cohesive team. Recall that a strong team is a cohesive unit striving for a shared objective rather than merely a group of individuals.

OBTAINING RESOURCES and Funding

Building a successful enterprise requires securing resources and money. Even the most inventive ideas may find it difficult to gain traction in the absence of sufficient funding and resources. We will look at a number of approaches and methods in this part for getting money and resources to support your entrepreneurial endeavors.

Recognizing the Landscape of Funding

It is crucial to comprehend the financial environment before delving into the various funding alternatives available. There are many different types of funding sources in the ecosystem, from more established ones like banks and venture capitalists to more recent ones like angel investors and crowdsourcing. Every financing source has pros and downsides of its own, so you must choose which one best suits the requirements and objectives of your project.

Customary Sources of Funding

Conventional financing sources comprise venture capitalists (VCs), who invest in high-potential firms in return for stock, and banks, who provide loans and credit lines. Typically, these sources need a strong business strategy, a track record of accomplishment, and an obvious route to financial success. They can offer substantial financial help, but they also frequently come with strict guidelines and a loss of decision-making authority.

Angel Capitalists

Angel investors are those who lend money to start-ups in return for stock. Angel investors, as opposed to VCs, are frequently more ready to take on risk in early-stage businesses. In addition to financial assistance, they may provide invaluable industry knowledge and contacts. Developing a connection with angel investors may be advantageous since they may end up being champions and long-term partners for your business.

Using crowdsourcing

In recent years, crowdsourcing has become more and more popular as a means of raising money from a huge number of people, usually via internet platforms. It enables business owners to present their concepts and win over a large audience to their cause. Using crowdfunding to verify your idea, make early sales, and create a following for your business may be quite successful. To stand out from the competition, though, you need a gripping narrative, a skillfully designed campaign, and a robust web presence.

Government Initiatives and Awards

Numerous nations provide funds and initiatives to encourage entrepreneurship and innovation. These programs give entrepreneurs funding, resources, and mentorship in an effort to promote economic expansion and job creation. Entrepreneurs can avail themselves of several forms of government help such as tax advantages, awards for innovation, and grants for research and development. Investigating these possibilities can reduce financial risks and give your business a big boost.

Creating an Alluring Funding Request

Create a strong fundraising application after you have determined which funding sources best suit the requirements of your project. Having a well-crafted proposal will greatly improve your chances of getting the money and resources you need. Some important components to think about when drafting your financing request are as follows:

A concise and lucid executive summary

The executive summary, which presents an overview of your endeavor, is the first section of your proposal. Your company proposal should be succinctly and persuasively summarized, emphasizing its distinct value proposition, market potential, and growth plan. To get the attention of possible funders or investors, make sure your content is interesting, succinct, and clear.

Comprehensive Business Strategy

To prove the viability and future profitability of your firm, you must have a thorough business plan. A thorough description of your good or service, a study of your target market, a list of your competitors, a marketing and sales plan, financial predictions, and a clear expansion strategy should all be included. Make sure you structure and explain your proposal logically, backing up your statements with facts and figures.

Projections of finances and ROI (return on investment)

Funders and investors are curious about your venture's financial prospects. Provide comprehensive financial predictions, including cash flow statements, expense breakdowns, and revenue estimates. Emphasize the anticipated return on investment and give evidence of how their support will help your business expand and become profitable. When preparing your estimates, be honest and practical because obtaining finance depends on your trustworthiness.

Group and Proficiency

In addition to ideas, financiers and investors also put money into the people who create them. Emphasize the credentials, background, and proficiency of your team members. Highlight their successes and pertinent experience that make them a good fit to carry out the plan for your venture. Showcase any mentors or advisers who are helping you with your project as well, since their legitimacy will strengthen your proposal.

Advantages over competitors and distinctive selling proposition

Clearly state the unique selling proposition (USP) of your business and how it sets you apart from rivals. Emphasize any patents, private technologies, or intellectual property that offers you a competitive edge. Stressing your unique selling point can help you attract investors and funders who are seeking for businesses that provide something fresh and creative to the market.

Developing Connections and Networking

It frequently takes more than just filing a financing request to get funds and resources. Developing contacts and a network with possible funders, investors, and business leaders may greatly improve your chances of success. Here are some tactics to think about:

Attend conferences and networking events

Attending conferences and networking events offers great chance to meet funders, investors, and business experts. Participate in discussions and attend pertinent events in your field. Prepare yourself to present your idea clearly and convincingly, and constantly maintain the connection by getting in touch with the people you spoke with afterwards.

Assist Accelerators and Incubators

Organizations that offer resources, mentorship, and assistance to businesses are known as incubators and accelerators. They can assist you in making connections with possible funding sources since they frequently have established networks of investors. Getting involved with an incubator or accelerator may boost your awareness in the startup community and offer helpful advice.

Make Use of Online and Social Media Channels

Online platforms and social media are effective tools for networking and connection development. Make use of industry-specific forums, LinkedIn, Twitter, and other platforms to establish connections with possible funders and investors. Provide updates on your project, participate in pertinent conversations, and highlight your experience to draw interest and establish credibility.

Seek guidance and mentorship.

When starting a business, mentors and advisers may offer invaluable advice and contacts. Seek out seasoned professionals that have developed successful businesses or are knowledgeable about your sector. Their contacts and insights may be quite helpful in obtaining money and resources.

3.5.4 Efficient Resource Management

For your enterprise to succeed over the long run, managing resources well is just as vital as securing money. The following tactics can be used to guarantee effective resource management:

Financial Planning and Budgeting

Create a thorough financial strategy and budget to efficiently track and manage your resources. To maximize resource allocation, evaluate and update your financial estimates on a regular basis, keep an eye on cash flow, and make well-informed judgments. To simplify the procedure, think about utilizing software and instruments for financial administration.

Setting priorities and focusing

Setting priorities and concentrating on tasks that support the objectives of your enterprise are essential when dealing with limited resources. Determine which important issues need to be addressed right now and devote resources appropriately. Refrain from overcommitting to too many undertakings at once to avoid wearing yourself out. Rather, focus on a small number of important tasks and do them effectively.

Cooperation and Joint Ventures

Working together with key partners might provide you access to more resources and knowledge. Seek alliances with businesses or groups that have comparable endeavors and similar target markets or objectives. Sharing expenses and pooling resources can be advantageous to both parties and hasten progress.

Ongoing Education and Adjustment

Entrepreneurship and innovation are dynamic processes that need for ongoing learning and adjustment. Keep abreast with market shifts, industry trends, and new technological developments. To guarantee best resource utilization and preserve a competitive edge, it is imperative to consistently assess and improve your strategy.

In conclusion, obtaining capital and resources is an essential part of creating a profitable business. Gaining the assistance you need for your entrepreneurial journey involves a number of critical stages, including knowing the financing environment, creating an appealing fundraising request, networking and forming partnerships, and efficiently managing resources. Through the utilization of various financing sources, a well-crafted proposal, and efficient resource management, you may release your creative spirit and steer your business toward sustained success.

Regulatory and Legal Aspects

It is essential to comprehend and abide by the legal and regulatory regulations that oversee your sector when launching a new business. If you don't, you risk paying hefty penalties, getting into legal trouble, and maybe losing your company. We will go over the main legal and regulatory factors that business owners should be mindful of in this part as they develop their enterprises.

Selecting the Appropriate Legal Framework

Selecting the appropriate legal form for your firm is among the first choices you must make. Your choice of legal structure will affect your business's governance, tax requirements, and personal accountability. Limited liability companies (LLCs), corporations, partnerships, and sole proprietorships are the most popular legal forms for small enterprises.

The most basic type of business ownership is a sole proprietorship, in which one person owns and runs the whole company. Being the only owner gives you total control over your company, but it also means that you are individually responsible for any debts and liabilities.

A partnership is a type of legal arrangement in which two or more people jointly own and manage a firm. All partners in a general partnership are equally liable for the obligations of the company. Both general partners, who have unlimited responsibility, and limited partners, who have limited liability, are present in a limited partnership.

Limited Liability Company (LLC): An LLC is a type of hybrid organization that combines the tax benefits and flexibility of a partnership with the limited liability protection of a corporation. The income and losses of the business can be carried over to the owners' personal tax returns, and as an LLC owner, you are not personally responsible for the obligations of the business.

Corporation: A corporation is an independent legal body distinct from its stockholders, who are its owners. The company has its own legal rights and duties, and the responsibility of the stockholders is restricted. More intricate legal and regulatory obligations apply to corporations, such as the need to keep corporate documents and conduct frequent shareholder meetings.

Various considerations, such as the type of your firm, the number of owners, and your long-term goals, will determine the best legal structure for your operation. To find the best legal structure for your unique situation, it is advised that you speak with a business adviser or legal expert.

Getting Your Company Registered

After deciding on a legal structure, you must register your company with the relevant government agencies. Depending on your area and the kind of business you are launching, the registration procedure may change. The following are typical procedures for registering a business:

Business Name Registration: Select a memorable and distinctive name for your company and make sure it is available. You will have to register your business name with the relevant government agency in many areas.

Getting an Employer Identification Number (EIN): In the US, the Internal Revenue Service (IRS) issues EINs, which are distinctive nine-digit numbers. For tax purposes, it serves as your company's identification. Getting an EIN is frequently necessary in order to create a company bank account and file taxes, even if you don't employ anyone.

Getting Licenses and permissions: In order to function lawfully, you might need to get certain licenses and permissions, depending on your area and business. Zoning permissions, health and safety permits, and professional licenses are a few examples. Do your homework on industry needs and make sure you abide by all applicable laws.

Tax Registration: Ascertain your company's tax responsibilities and register with the relevant tax authorities. This might entail setting up accounts for income tax, payroll tax, and sales tax. To be sure you comprehend and abide by all tax obligations, get advice from a tax expert.

Getting Business Insurance: To shield your endeavor from possible hazards and liabilities, think about getting business insurance. Property insurance, professional liability insurance, and general liability insurance are common forms of company insurance. To get the best coverage for your company, speak with an insurance representative.

Protection of Intellectual Property

Creative works of the mind, including innovations, designs, trademarks, and copyrights, are referred to as intellectual property (IP). It's critical to protect your intellectual property if you want to keep people from stealing your creative ideas. Here are some essential types of protection for intellectual property:

Patents: When an inventor creates a novel and practical invention, they are granted exclusive rights to it. It offers legal defense against unauthorized production, use, or sale of the innovation. You must fulfill certain requirements for patentability and submit a patent application to the relevant patent office in order to receive a patent.

Trademarks: A trademark is an identifying mark, like a logo or brand name, that sets your goods and services apart from those of competitors. Getting a trademark registered gives you legal protection and stops other people from utilizing marks that are confusing to customers.

Copyrights: Original works of authorship, such as compositions in music, painting, or literature, are protected by copyright laws. It gives the author the only authority to copy, share, and exhibit the work. Although copyright is automatically protected at the time of creation, you can enhance your legal rights by registering your copyright with the relevant copyright office.

Trade secrets are important and exclusive company knowledge that provides a competitive edge to your enterprise. Customer lists, production procedures, and marketing plans are a few examples. Implementing security measures, like as non-disclosure agreements and restricted access to sensitive information, is necessary to protect trade secrets.

Being aware of and safeguarding your intellectual property is essential to keeping a competitive advantage in the market. To evaluate your IP assets and create a plan for their protection, speak with an intellectual property lawyer.

Respect for Regulations

Adhering to industry-specific rules and regulations is a necessary part of running a firm. You risk serious penalties and reputational harm if you don't follow these requirements. The following are important aspects of regulatory compliance to think about:

Employment Laws: Make sure you abide by labor laws, such as those pertaining to minimum pay requirements, overtime restrictions, and workplace safety rules. Learn about the rules pertaining to job discrimination and make sure that workers are treated fairly.

Data Protection and Privacy: You are required to abide by regulations pertaining to data protection and privacy if your company gathers and maintains client data. This entails getting permission before collecting data, putting security measures in place to safeguard client information, and being open and honest about the use of data.

Environmental standards: To reduce the negative effects of your company's operations on the environment, you might have to abide by environmental standards, depending on your industry. This might entail managing trash disposal, securing licenses, and putting sustainable policies into action.

Advertising and Marketing rules: Make sure that the rules pertaining to misleading advertising, false advertising, and consumer protection are followed in your advertising and marketing campaigns. Learn about the rules that apply to your business, such as those that control financial services or pharmaceutical advertising.

Product Safety and Quality criteria: You have to abide by these criteria if your company produces or distributes goods. This involves making certain that the labels on your items adhere to the relevant safety standards.

For enterprises, being up to date on regulatory changes and upholding compliance are constant responsibilities. To keep informed about the most recent laws and industry best practices, think about contacting industry groups or getting legal counsel.

Having a solid understanding of and adherence to legal and regulatory matters is crucial to the success of any endeavor. You may reduce risks and set yourself up for long-term success by selecting the best legal structure, registering your company, safeguarding your intellectual property, and making sure you're in compliance with all regulations. It is advisable to get advice from legal experts and industry specialists in order to effectively traverse the intricate web of legal and regulatory obligations.

Executing
Your Innovative Ideas

Effective project management

E ffective project management is a critical component of turning innovative ideas into successful ventures. It involves planning, organizing, and executing tasks and resources to achieve specific goals within a defined timeframe. In the context of innovation, project management plays a crucial role in ensuring that innovative ideas are implemented efficiently and effectively.

The Importance of Project Management in Innovation

INNOVATION IS NOT JUST about coming up with great ideas; it is about executing those ideas and bringing them to market. Without effective project management, even the most brilliant ideas can fail to materialize or fall short of their potential. Project management provides a structured approach to managing the various aspects of an innovation project, including time, resources, and risks.

One of the key benefits of project management in innovation is that it helps ensure that innovative ideas are implemented in a systematic and organized manner. It helps to break down complex projects into manageable tasks, set clear objectives, and allocate resources effectively. By doing so, project management enables teams to stay focused, meet deadlines, and deliver high-quality outcomes.

The project management process

THE PROJECT MANAGEMENT process consists of several stages that guide the execution of an innovation project. These stages include:

Project Initiation

THE PROJECT INITIATION stage involves defining the project's objectives, scope, and deliverables. It is essential to clearly articulate the problem the project aims to solve and the desired outcomes. This stage also involves identifying key stakeholders and establishing their roles and responsibilities.

Project Planning

DURING THE PROJECT planning stage, the project manager and the team develop a detailed plan that outlines the tasks, timelines, and resources required to achieve the project's objectives. This plan serves as a roadmap for the project and helps ensure that everyone is aligned and working towards a common goal.

Project Execution

THE PROJECT EXECUTION stage is where the actual work takes place. The project manager oversees the implementation of the project plan, assigns tasks to team members, and monitors progress. Effective communication and collaboration are crucial during this stage to ensure that everyone is on the same page and any issues or roadblocks are addressed promptly.

Project Monitoring and Control

THROUGHOUT THE PROJECT, it is essential to monitor progress and control any deviations from the plan. This involves tracking key performance indicators, assessing risks, and making necessary adjustments to keep the project on track. Regular status updates and meetings help keep stakeholders informed and ensure that any changes or issues are addressed in a timely manner.

Project Closure

THE PROJECT CLOSURE stage marks the completion of the project. It involves evaluating the project's success against the defined objectives, documenting lessons learned, and celebrating achievements. This stage also includes transitioning the project's outcomes to the appropriate stakeholders and conducting a post-project review to identify areas for improvement.

Key Principles of Effective Project Management

TO ENSURE EFFECTIVE project management in the context of innovation, it is important to adhere to certain key principles. These principles include:

Clear Communication

CLEAR AND OPEN COMMUNICATION is vital for successful project management. It ensures that all team members understand their roles and responsibilities, have access to relevant information, and can collaborate effectively. Regular communication channels, such as team meetings and progress updates, help keep everyone informed and aligned.

Flexibility and adaptability

INNOVATION PROJECTS often involve uncertainty and change. Effective project management requires flexibility and adaptability to respond to unexpected challenges and opportunities. Being open to adjusting plans, reallocating resources, and embracing new ideas is crucial for navigating the dynamic nature of innovation.

Risk Management

INNOVATION PROJECTS inherently involve risks. Effective project management involves identifying and assessing risks early on and developing strategies to mitigate them. This includes contingency planning, regular risk assessments, and proactive problem-solving to minimize the impact of potential risks on the project's success.

Collaboration and teamwork

SUCCESSFUL PROJECT management relies on effective collaboration and teamwork. Building a strong and cohesive team, fostering a culture of trust and collaboration, and encouraging open communication are essential for achieving project goals. Collaboration tools and techniques, such as project management software and regular team meetings, can facilitate effective teamwork.

Continuous Improvement

CONTINUOUS IMPROVEMENT is a fundamental principle of effective project management. Regularly evaluating project performance, learning from successes and failures, and implementing improvements are essential for enhancing project outcomes. This includes capturing lessons learned, implementing best practices, and applying feedback to future projects.

Tools and Techniques for Effective Project Management

SEVERAL TOOLS AND TECHNIQUES can support effective project management in the context of innovation. These include:

Project Management Software

PROJECT MANAGEMENT software provides a centralized platform for planning, organizing, and tracking project activities. It allows teams to create and manage project schedules, allocate resources, track progress, and collaborate effectively. Popular project management software includes tools like Asana, Trello, and Microsoft Project.

Agile Methodology

AGILE METHODOLOGY IS a project management approach that emphasizes flexibility, collaboration, and iterative development. It is particularly well-suited for innovation projects that require frequent adjustments and rapid prototyping. Agile methodologies, such as Scrum and Kanban, enable teams to deliver value incrementally and respond to changing requirements.

Risk management techniques

VARIOUS RISK MANAGEMENT techniques can help identify, assess, and mitigate risks in innovation projects. These techniques include risk identification workshops, risk registers, risk impact and probability assessments, and risk response planning. By proactively managing risks, project managers can minimize potential disruptions and ensure project success.

Performance Metrics and Key Performance Indicators (Kpis)

PERFORMANCE METRICS and KPIs provide objective measures of project progress and success. They help project managers track performance, identify areas for improvement, and make data-driven decisions. Examples of project KPIs include project timeline adherence, budget variance, customer satisfaction ratings, and product quality metrics.

Effective project management is essential for turning innovative ideas into successful ventures. By following a structured project management process, adhering to key principles, and utilizing appropriate tools and techniques, entrepreneurs can increase the likelihood of project success. Project management provides the framework and guidance needed to navigate the complexities of innovation and bring ideas to life.

Developing a Minimum Viable Product (MVP)

I n the world of entrepreneurship and innovation, developing a minimum viable product (MVP) is a crucial step towards success. An MVP is a version of your product or service that has just enough features to satisfy early customers and gather feedback for future iterations. It allows you to test your ideas, validate assumptions, and make informed decisions about the direction of your venture.

Understanding the Concept of Minimum Viable Product

THE CONCEPT OF A MINIMUM viable product was popularized by Eric Ries in his book "The Lean Startup." Ries defines an MVP as "that version of a new product that allows a team to collect the maximum amount of validated learning about customers with the least effort." In other words, an MVP is not the final product but a starting point that helps you learn and iterate.

The key idea behind an MVP is to avoid spending excessive time and resources on building a fully-featured product before testing it in the market. By focusing on the core value proposition and essential features, you can quickly get your product into the hands of early adopters and gather valuable feedback to guide your development process.

Identifying the Core Value Proposition

BEFORE DEVELOPING AN MVP, it is crucial to identify and define your core value proposition. The core value proposition is the unique benefit or advantage that your product or service offers to customers. It is what sets you apart from competitors and provides value to your target market.

To identify your core value proposition, you need to understand your customers' pain points, needs, and desires. Conduct market research, gather customer feedback, and analyze the competitive landscape to gain insights into what customers truly value. Once you have a clear understanding of your core value proposition, you can prioritize the features and functionalities that will deliver that value.

Defining the Scope of Your MVP

ONCE YOU HAVE IDENTIFIED your core value proposition, it is time to define the scope of your MVP. The scope refers to the set of features and functionalities that will be included in the initial version of your product. It is essential to strike a balance between providing enough value to attract early customers and keeping the scope manageable to avoid unnecessary complexity.

To define the scope of your MVP, consider the following factors:

Core Features: Identify the features that are essential to delivering your core value proposition. These features should address the most critical pain points of your target customers.

User Experience: Focus on creating a seamless and intuitive user experience. Keep the user interface simple and easy to navigate, ensuring that users can quickly understand and use your product.

Technical Feasibility: Consider the technical feasibility of implementing the features within the given time and resource constraints. Avoid overly complex or resource-intensive features that may delay the development process.

Feedback Mechanisms: Incorporate feedback mechanisms into your MVP to gather insights from early adopters. This can include surveys, user testing, or direct communication channels to collect feedback and iterate on your product.

By carefully defining the scope of your MVP, you can ensure that you are delivering value to your customers while keeping the development process efficient and focused.

Building and Testing Your MVP

ONCE YOU HAVE DEFINED the scope of your MVP, it is time to start building and testing. The development process should follow an iterative approach, where you continuously build, test, and learn from each iteration.

Here are some key steps to consider when building and testing your MVP:

Prototype Development: Start by creating a basic prototype that demonstrates the core features and functionalities of your product. This can be a simple mockup, wireframe, or even a clickable prototype that allows users to interact with your product.

User Testing: Conduct user testing sessions with a small group of target customers. Observe how they interact with your product, gather feedback, and identify areas for improvement. User testing provides valuable insights into usability, functionality, and the overall user experience.

Iterative Development: Based on the feedback received from user testing, iterate on your MVP by refining existing features, adding new features, or removing unnecessary ones. Each iteration should bring you closer to a product that meets the needs and expectations of your target market.

Continuous Learning: Throughout the development process, embrace a culture of continuous learning. Analyze the feedback and data collected from each iteration and use them to inform your decision-making. Be open to pivoting or making significant changes based on the insights gained.

Validation: As you iterate and improve your MVP, aim to validate your assumptions and hypotheses. Use metrics and data to measure the impact of your product on customers and the market. This validation process will help you make informed decisions about the future direction of your venture.

Gathering Feedback and Iterating

ONE OF THE PRIMARY purposes of developing an MVP is to gather feedback from early adopters and use it to iterate and improve your product. Feedback is a valuable source of insights that can help you refine your value proposition, enhance the user experience, and address any shortcomings in your offering.

To gather feedback effectively, consider the following strategies:

User Surveys: Create surveys to gather feedback on various aspects of your product, such as usability, features, and overall satisfaction. Keep the surveys concise and focused to encourage higher response rates.

User Interviews: Conduct one-on-one interviews with early adopters to gain deeper insights into their experiences and expectations. Ask open-ended questions and encourage participants to share their thoughts, suggestions, and pain points.

Analytics and Metrics: Utilize analytics tools to track user behavior, engagement, and conversion rates. Analyze the data to identify patterns, trends, and areas for improvement.

Customer Support Channels: Establish direct communication channels, such as email or live chat, to encourage customers to provide feedback and report any issues they encounter. Respond promptly to customer inquiries and use their feedback to drive improvements.

By actively seeking and incorporating feedback into your development process, you can ensure that your product evolves based on the needs and preferences of your target market.

Balancing Speed and Quality

WHEN DEVELOPING AN MVP, it is essential to strike a balance between speed and quality. While it is crucial to move quickly and get your product into the hands of customers, you should not compromise on the quality of the user experience or the core value proposition.

To balance speed and quality, consider the following strategies:

Prioritize: Focus on the features and functionalities that are critical to delivering your core value proposition. Avoid getting caught up in unnecessary details or features that can be added in later iterations.

Iterate: Embrace an iterative approach to development, where you continuously build, test, and learn from each iteration. This allows you to make incremental improvements while maintaining a fast pace.

Test Early and Often: Conduct user testing and gather feedback as early as possible in the development process. This helps identify any usability issues or gaps in the value proposition before investing significant time and resources.

Maintain a Minimum Viable Experience: While an MVP may not have all the bells and whistles of a fully-featured product, it should still provide a satisfactory user experience. Ensure that the core features are functional, intuitive, and meet the needs of your target customers.

By finding the right balance between speed and quality, you can develop an MVP that not only meets the needs of your customers but also allows you to iterate and improve efficiently.

Developing a Minimum Viable Product (MVP) is a critical step in the journey of building a successful venture. It allows you to test your ideas, validate assumptions, and gather feedback from early adopters. By understanding the concept of an MVP, identifying your core value proposition, defining the scope, and following an iterative development process, you can create a product that meets the needs of your target market while balancing speed and quality. Remember, an MVP is not the final product but a starting point for continuous learning and improvement. Embrace feedback, iterate, and use the insights gained to drive the success of your venture.

Iterative development and continuous improvement

Innovation is not a one-time event; it is an ongoing process that requires constant refinement and improvement. Iterative development and continuous improvement are essential components of this process, allowing entrepreneurs to adapt and evolve their ideas and ventures over time. By embracing these principles, entrepreneurs can enhance their chances of success and stay ahead in today's rapidly changing business landscape.

The Power of Iterative Development

ITERATIVE DEVELOPMENT is a methodical approach to building and refining a product or service through a series of incremental steps. Instead of attempting to create a perfect solution from the start, entrepreneurs focus on developing a minimum viable product (MVP) and then gathering feedback from users or customers. This feedback is then used to inform the next iteration of the product, which is built upon the previous version, incorporating improvements and addressing any identified issues.

The power of iterative development lies in its ability to reduce risk and increase the likelihood of success. By releasing an MVP early on, entrepreneurs can validate their assumptions and test the market demand for their product or service. This early feedback allows them to make informed decisions about the direction of their venture, ensuring that they are building something that meets the needs of their target audience.

Iterative development also enables entrepreneurs to be agile and responsive to changes in the market. By continuously iterating and improving their product, they can quickly adapt to new trends, customer preferences, and emerging technologies. This flexibility is crucial in today's fast-paced business environment, where staying ahead of the competition requires constant innovation and adaptation.

The Continuous Improvement Mindset

CONTINUOUS IMPROVEMENT is a mindset that drives entrepreneurs to constantly seek ways to enhance their products, processes, and overall business performance. It involves a commitment to learning, experimentation, and embracing feedback as a valuable source of insights and opportunities for growth.

To cultivate a continuous improvement mindset, entrepreneurs should foster a culture of learning within their organization. This can be achieved by encouraging employees to share their ideas, providing opportunities for professional development, and creating a safe space for experimentation and risk-taking. By promoting a growth mindset, entrepreneurs can empower their team members to embrace change and actively contribute to the improvement of the venture.

Feedback plays a crucial role in the continuous improvement process. Entrepreneurs should actively seek feedback from customers, employees, and other stakeholders to gain valuable insights into areas that require improvement. This feedback can be obtained through surveys, interviews, user testing, and other feedback mechanisms. By listening to their customers and stakeholders, entrepreneurs can identify pain points, uncover unmet needs, and make data-driven decisions to enhance their products or services.

In addition to external feedback, entrepreneurs should also encourage self-reflection and self-assessment. By regularly evaluating their own performance and seeking opportunities for growth, entrepreneurs can identify areas where they can improve their skills, knowledge, and capabilities. This self-awareness is essential for personal and professional development, enabling entrepreneurs to become more effective leaders and innovators.

Implementing Iterative Development and Continuous Improvement

TO EFFECTIVELY IMPLEMENT iterative development and continuous improvement in their ventures, entrepreneurs should follow a structured approach. Here are some key steps to consider:

Define clear goals and metrics: Before embarking on the iterative development process, entrepreneurs should clearly define their goals and establish metrics to measure success. These goals and metrics will serve as a guide throughout the iterative development journey, helping entrepreneurs stay focused and track their progress.

Build a feedback loop: Establishing a feedback loop is crucial for gathering insights and feedback from customers, users, and stakeholders. This can be done through various channels, such as surveys, user testing, focus groups, and social media listening. By actively seeking feedback, entrepreneurs can identify areas for improvement and make informed decisions about the next iteration of their product or service.

Prioritize and plan: Based on the feedback received, entrepreneurs should prioritize the areas that require improvement and plan the next iteration of their product or service. This involves identifying the most critical issues to address, setting clear objectives for the next iteration, and allocating resources accordingly.

Execute and test: Once the plan is in place, entrepreneurs should execute the next iteration of their product or service and test it with their target audience. This may involve releasing a new version of the product, implementing new features, or making changes to the existing offering. The key is to gather feedback and data to evaluate the impact of the changes made.

Analyze and learn: After the new iteration has been tested, entrepreneurs should analyze the results and learn from the feedback received. This involves evaluating the impact of the changes made, identifying areas of success, and identifying areas that still require improvement. By analyzing the data and insights gathered, entrepreneurs can make informed decisions about the next steps in the iterative development process.

Repeat and refine: The iterative development process is cyclical, with each iteration building upon the previous one. Entrepreneurs should repeat the process, incorporating the lessons learned from each iteration and refining their product or service based on the feedback received. This continuous cycle of improvement allows entrepreneurs to create products that are better aligned with market needs and customer preferences.

By embracing iterative development and continuous improvement, entrepreneurs can unlock the full potential of their innovative ideas and build ventures that are adaptable, resilient, and successful in the long run. It is through this iterative process that entrepreneurs can refine their products, optimize their operations, and stay ahead of the competition in today's dynamic business landscape.

Managing Risks and Uncertainties

Innovation and entrepreneurship are inherently risky endeavors. As an entrepreneur, you will face numerous uncertainties and challenges along the way. However, by effectively managing risks and uncertainties, you can increase the likelihood of success for your innovative venture. In this section, we will explore strategies and techniques to help you navigate the unpredictable nature of entrepreneurship.

Identifying and Assessing Risks

THE FIRST STEP IN MANAGING risks is to identify and assess potential risks that may impact your venture. Risks can come in various forms, such as financial risks, market risks, operational risks, and legal risks. By conducting a thorough risk assessment, you can gain a better understanding of the potential challenges that lie ahead.

To identify risks, consider conducting a SWOT analysis (Strengths, Weaknesses, Opportunities, and Threats) for your venture. This analysis will help you identify both internal and external factors that may pose risks to your business. Additionally, consider seeking input from experts and industry professionals who can provide valuable insights into potential risks specific to your industry.

Once risks are identified, it is important to assess their potential impact and likelihood of occurrence. This can be done by assigning a risk rating to each identified risk, taking into account factors such as severity, probability, and potential mitigation strategies. By prioritizing risks based on their potential impact, you can allocate resources and develop appropriate risk management strategies.

Developing Risk Mitigation Strategies

AFTER IDENTIFYING AND assessing risks, the next step is to develop risk mitigation strategies. These strategies aim to minimize the impact of risks and increase the likelihood of success for your venture. Here are some common risk-mitigating strategies:

Diversification: Diversifying your product or service offerings can help mitigate the risk of relying too heavily on a single revenue stream. By offering a range of products or services, you can spread the risk and reduce the impact of market fluctuations.

Insurance: Depending on the nature of your venture, obtaining appropriate insurance coverage can help protect against potential financial losses. Insurance options may include general liability insurance, professional liability insurance, and product liability insurance, among others.

Contingency Planning: Developing contingency plans can help you prepare for unexpected events or disruptions. These plans outline alternative courses of action to be taken in the event of a risk materializing. By having contingency plans in place, you can minimize the impact of risks and ensure business continuity.

Strategic Partnerships: Collaborating with strategic partners can help mitigate risks by leveraging their expertise, resources, and networks. Strategic partnerships can provide access to new markets, shared costs and risks, and increased credibility.

Financial Planning: Effective financial planning is crucial for managing risks. This includes creating realistic financial projections, maintaining adequate cash reserves, and regularly monitoring and adjusting your financial strategies based on market conditions.

Legal Compliance: Ensuring compliance with relevant laws and regulations is essential for managing legal risks. This may involve consulting with legal professionals to understand and navigate the legal landscape specific to your industry.

Continuous Monitoring and Evaluation: Risk management is an ongoing process. It is important to continuously monitor and evaluate the effectiveness of your risk mitigation strategies. Regularly reviewing and updating your risk management plans will help you stay proactive and responsive to changing circumstances.

Embracing Uncertainty and Adaptability

WHILE MANAGING RISKS is important, it is equally crucial to embrace uncertainty and be adaptable in the face of unforeseen challenges. The entrepreneurial journey is filled with uncertainties, and being able to adapt and pivot when necessary is key to long-term success.

To embrace uncertainty and foster adaptability, consider the following strategies:

Cultivate a Growth Mindset: Adopt a mindset that views challenges and failures as opportunities for growth and learning. Embrace a willingness to experiment, iterate, and adapt your strategies based on feedback and market dynamics.

Foster a Culture of Innovation: Encourage your team to think creatively and embrace change. Create an environment that values and rewards innovation, and empower your employees to take calculated risks and explore new ideas.

Stay Connected: Build a strong network of mentors, advisors, and industry peers who can provide guidance and support. Engage in industry events, conferences, and networking opportunities to stay informed about emerging trends and best practices.

Monitor Market Trends: Stay abreast of market trends and disruptions that may impact your industry. By monitoring market dynamics, you can proactively identify potential risks and opportunities and adjust your strategies accordingly.

Agility and Flexibility: Be prepared to pivot and adapt your business model or strategies based on changing market conditions. This may involve revisiting your value proposition, target market, or distribution channels to stay relevant and competitive.

By effectively managing risks and embracing uncertainty, you can navigate the unpredictable nature of entrepreneurship and increase the likelihood of success for your innovative venture. Remember, innovation requires taking calculated risks, and by implementing sound risk management strategies, you can unleash your inner innovator and build a successful and sustainable venture.

**Marketing and Branding
Strategies for Innovation**

Understanding Your Target Market

In order to successfully market and sell your innovative product or service, it is crucial to have a deep understanding of your target market. Your target market consists of a specific group of individuals or businesses that are most likely to be interested in and purchase your offering. By understanding their needs, preferences, and behaviors, you can tailor your marketing efforts to effectively reach and engage with them.

Defining Your Target Market

BEFORE YOU CAN UNDERSTAND your target market, you must first define it. This involves identifying the characteristics and demographics of the individuals or businesses that are most likely to benefit from and be interested in your innovation. Some key factors to consider when defining your target market include:

Demographics: This includes factors such as age, gender, income level, education level, and geographic location. Understanding the demographic profile of your target market can help you tailor your marketing messages and channels to effectively reach them.

Psychographics: Psychographics refer to the attitudes, values, interests, and lifestyles of your target market. By understanding their psychographic profile, you can create marketing campaigns that resonate with their beliefs and motivations.

Behaviors: Analyzing the behaviors of your target market can provide valuable insights into their purchasing habits, media consumption, and online behavior. This information can help you determine the best channels and strategies to reach and engage with them.

Needs and Pain Points: Understanding the needs and pain points of your target market is crucial for developing a product or service that addresses their specific challenges. By identifying their needs, you can position your innovation as a solution that meets their requirements.

Conducting Market Research

ONCE YOU HAVE DEFINED your target market, it is important to conduct thorough market research to gather data and insights that will inform your marketing strategy. Market research involves collecting and analyzing information about your target market, competitors, and industry trends. Here are some key steps to conducting effective market research:

Surveys and Interviews: Surveys and interviews are valuable tools for gathering primary data directly from your target market. By asking specific questions, you can gain insights into their preferences, needs, and behaviors.

Secondary Research: Secondary research involves gathering existing data and information from reliable sources such as industry reports, government publications, and market research studies. This can provide valuable insights into market trends, competitor analysis, and consumer behavior.

Competitor Analysis: Analyzing your competitors can help you identify gaps in the market and differentiate your offering. By understanding their strengths, weaknesses, and marketing strategies, you can position your innovation more effectively.

Trends and Forecasting: Keeping up with industry trends and forecasting future developments can help you stay ahead of the curve. By understanding emerging technologies, consumer preferences, and market shifts, you can adapt your marketing strategy to capitalize on new opportunities.

Segmenting Your Target Market

SEGMENTING YOUR TARGET market involves dividing it into distinct groups based on shared characteristics or behaviors. This allows you to tailor your marketing efforts to each segment's specific needs and preferences. Here are some common segmentation strategies:

Demographic Segmentation: This involves dividing your target market based on demographic factors such as age, gender, income, and education. For example, a skincare brand may target different age groups with specific products and messaging.

Psychographic Segmentation: Psychographic segmentation involves dividing your target market based on their attitudes, values, and lifestyles. This can help you create marketing campaigns that resonate with their beliefs and motivations.

Behavioral Segmentation: Behavioral segmentation divides your target market based on their purchasing habits, usage patterns, and brand loyalty. This can help you identify high-value customers and tailor your marketing efforts to retain and upsell them.

Geographic Segmentation: Geographic segmentation involves dividing your target market based on their geographic location. This can be useful for businesses that have different offerings or marketing strategies for different regions.

Targeting and Positioning

ONCE YOU HAVE SEGMENTED your target market, you can then determine which segments to prioritize and target with your marketing efforts. Targeting involves selecting the segments that are most likely to be interested in and purchase your innovation. Positioning, on the other hand, involves creating a unique value proposition and positioning your offering in a way that differentiates it from competitors.

To effectively target and position your innovation, consider the following:

Value Proposition: Clearly articulate the unique value that your innovation offers to your target market. This could be a specific problem it solves, a benefit it provides, or a competitive advantage it has over alternatives.

Messaging and Communication: Develop compelling messaging and communication strategies that resonate with your target market. This includes crafting persuasive marketing messages and selecting the most effective channels to reach and engage with them.

Differentiation: Differentiate your innovation from competitors by highlighting its unique features, benefits, or positioning. This can help you stand out in a crowded market and attract the attention of your target market.

By understanding your target market, conducting thorough market research, segmenting your audience, and effectively targeting and positioning your innovation, you can develop a marketing strategy that maximizes your chances of success. Remember, marketing is not a one-size-fits-all approach, and by tailoring your efforts to the specific needs and preferences of your target market, you can increase your chances of capturing their attention and driving sales.

Creating a Unique Value Proposition

In today's competitive business landscape, it is crucial for entrepreneurs to create a unique value proposition that sets their venture apart from the competition. A value proposition is a statement that clearly communicates the unique benefits and value that a product or service offers to its target customers. It is the foundation upon which a successful marketing strategy is built.

Understanding the Importance of a Unique Value Proposition

A UNIQUE VALUE PROPOSITION is essential for several reasons. Firstly, it helps entrepreneurs differentiate their venture from competitors in the market. With so many options available to consumers, having a clear and compelling value proposition can have a significant impact on their decision-making process.

Secondly, a unique value proposition helps entrepreneurs communicate the benefits and value of their product or service to their target audience effectively. It answers the question, "Why should customers choose your product or service over others?" By clearly articulating the unique benefits, entrepreneurs can attract and retain customers who resonate with their value proposition.

Lastly, a strong value proposition can also serve as a guiding principle for entrepreneurs when making strategic decisions. It helps them stay focused on their core offering and ensures that all aspects of their business align with their unique value proposition.

Identifying Your Unique Selling Points

TO CREATE A UNIQUE value proposition, entrepreneurs must first identify their unique selling points (USPs). These are the specific features, benefits, or characteristics that set their product or service apart from others in the market. Here are some steps to help entrepreneurs identify their USPs:

Conduct market research: Start by understanding the needs, preferences, and pain points of your target market. This will help you identify gaps in the market and opportunities for differentiation.

Analyze competitors: Study your competitors to identify their strengths and weaknesses. This will help you identify areas where you can differentiate yourself and offer something unique.

Identify Key Benefits: Determine the key benefits that your product or service offers to customers. These benefits should address the pain points of your target market and provide a solution that is superior to what competitors offer.

Assess Uniqueness: Evaluate how unique your identified benefits are in the market. If there are already similar offerings, consider how you can differentiate yourself further to create a truly unique value proposition.

Test and refine: Once you have identified your potential USPs, test them with your target audience to gather feedback. Use this feedback to refine and strengthen your value proposition.

Crafting Your Unique Value Proposition

ONCE YOU HAVE IDENTIFIED your unique selling points, it's time to craft your unique value proposition. Here are some key elements to consider when creating your value proposition:

Clear and Concise: Your value proposition should be clear, concise, and easy to understand. Avoid using jargon or technical language that may confuse your target audience.

Customer-centric: Focus on the benefits and value that your product or service provides to your customers. Highlight how it solves their problems or fulfills their needs.

Differentiation: Clearly communicate how your offering is different from competitors. Highlight the unique features, benefits, or characteristics that set you apart.

Quantifiable: Whenever possible, use specific numbers or data to quantify the benefits or results that customers can expect from your product or service. This adds credibility and helps customers understand the value they will receive.

Emotional Appeal: Consider incorporating emotional triggers into your value proposition. Appeal to the emotions and aspirations of your target audience to create a deeper connection.

Consistency: Ensure that your value proposition aligns with your overall brand and messaging. Consistency across all touchpoints will strengthen your brand identity and build trust with customers.

Communicating and Testing Your Value Proposition

ONCE YOU HAVE CRAFTED your unique value proposition, it's important to effectively communicate it to your target audience. Here are some strategies to consider:

Website and Landing Pages: Clearly articulate your value proposition on your website's homepage and landing pages. Use compelling headlines, subheadings, and visuals to grab attention and communicate your unique selling points.

Marketing Collateral: Incorporate your value proposition into your marketing materials, such as brochures, flyers, and advertisements. Ensure that it is prominently displayed and easily understood.

Social Media and Content Marketing: Leverage social media platforms and content marketing to communicate your value proposition. Create engaging and informative content that highlights the benefits and value you offer.

Customer Testimonials: Share testimonials and success stories from satisfied customers who have experienced the benefits of your product or service. This adds credibility and reinforces your value proposition.

A/B Testing: Conduct A/B testing to compare different versions of your value proposition and messaging. This will help you identify which resonates best with your target audience and refine your approach accordingly.

Remember, creating a unique value proposition is an ongoing process. As your venture evolves and the market changes, it's important to regularly reassess and refine your value proposition to stay relevant and competitive. By continuously focusing on delivering unique value to your customers, you can build a strong and successful venture.

Developing a marketing strategy

Once you have identified your target market and created a unique value proposition, it is time to develop a marketing strategy that will effectively promote your innovative product or service. A well-crafted marketing strategy will help you reach your target audience, generate awareness, and ultimately drive sales. In this section, we will explore the key components of developing a marketing strategy and provide you with practical tips to ensure its success.

Understanding Your Target Market

BEFORE DIVING INTO the specifics of your marketing strategy, it is crucial to have a deep understanding of your target market. This involves conducting thorough market research to identify your potential customers, their needs, preferences, and behaviors. By understanding your target market, you can tailor your marketing efforts to effectively reach and engage with them.

To gain insights into your target market, consider conducting surveys, interviews, or focus groups to gather valuable feedback. Analyze demographic data, such as age, gender, location, and income, to segment your target market and create targeted marketing campaigns. Additionally, explore psychographic factors, such as interests, values, and lifestyle choices, to further refine your marketing approach.

Setting clear marketing objectives

ONCE YOU HAVE A SOLID understanding of your target market, it is essential to set clear marketing objectives. These objectives will guide your marketing strategy and help you measure its success. Your marketing objectives should be specific, measurable, attainable, relevant, and time-bound (SMART). For example, your objective could be to increase brand awareness by 20% within the next six months or to generate 100 new leads per month.

By setting clear marketing objectives, you can align your marketing efforts with your overall business goals and track your progress along the way. Regularly evaluate and adjust your objectives as needed to ensure they remain relevant and achievable.

Choosing the Right Marketing Channels

WITH A CLEAR UNDERSTANDING of your target market and defined marketing objectives, it is time to choose the right marketing channels to reach your audience effectively. There are numerous marketing channels available, both online and offline, and selecting the most appropriate ones for your business is crucial.

Consider the preferences and behaviors of your target market when choosing marketing channels. For example, if your target market consists of tech-savvy individuals, digital marketing channels such as social media, search engine optimization (SEO), and email marketing may be effective. On the other hand, if your target market is more traditional, offline channels like print advertising, direct mail, or attending industry conferences may be more suitable.

It is important to note that a multi-channel approach is often the most effective. By utilizing a combination of online and offline channels, you can reach a wider audience and increase the chances of engaging with potential customers.

Crafting Compelling Marketing Messages

ONCE YOU HAVE CHOSEN your marketing channels, it is crucial to craft compelling marketing messages that resonate with your target market. Your marketing messages should clearly communicate the unique value proposition of your product or service and persuade potential customers to take action.

To create compelling marketing messages, consider the following tips:

Clearly articulate the benefits of your product or service. Highlight how your offering solves a problem or fulfills a need for your target market. Focus on the value it provides and how it can improve their lives or businesses.

Use persuasive language: Use persuasive language and storytelling techniques to capture the attention of your audience. Appeal to their emotions and demonstrate how your product or service can make a positive impact.

Differentiate yourself from competitors: Highlight what sets your product or service apart from competitors. Emphasize your unique features, quality, or customer service to position yourself as the superior choice.

Keep it concise and clear. Avoid using jargon or complex language that may confuse or alienate your audience. Keep your messages concise, clear, and easy to understand.

Test and refine your messages: Continuously test and refine your marketing messages to ensure they resonate with your target market. Conduct A/B testing, gather feedback, and make adjustments as needed to optimize your messaging.

Allocating Marketing Budget

DEVELOPING A MARKETING strategy requires allocating a budget to support your marketing efforts. Your marketing budget should be based on your overall business goals, marketing objectives, and the resources available to you. It is important to strike a balance between investing enough to achieve your marketing objectives and ensuring a positive return on investment (ROI).

Consider the following factors when allocating your marketing budget:

Prioritize marketing channels: Allocate a larger portion of your budget to the marketing channels that have proven to be most effective in reaching and engaging your target market.

Consider the customer acquisition cost (CAC): Calculate the cost of acquiring a new customer through each marketing channel. This will help you determine the most cost-effective channels and allocate your budget accordingly.

Monitor and adjust: Regularly monitor the performance of your marketing campaigns and adjust your budget allocation as needed. If a particular channel is not delivering the desired results, consider reallocating funds to more effective channels.

Invest in analytics and tracking tools: Allocate a portion of your budget to analytics and tracking tools that will help you measure the effectiveness of your marketing efforts. This will enable you to make data-driven decisions and optimize your marketing strategy over time.

Measuring and Evaluating Marketing Success

TO ENSURE THE EFFECTIVENESS of your marketing strategy, it is crucial to measure and evaluate its success. By tracking key performance indicators (KPIs), you can assess the impact of your marketing efforts and make data-driven decisions to optimize your strategy.

Some common marketing KPIs to consider include:

Conversion rate: Measure the percentage of website visitors or leads that convert into paying customers. This will help you assess the effectiveness of your marketing messages and channels.

Return on investment (ROI): Calculate the ROI of your marketing campaigns by comparing the revenue generated against the cost of your marketing efforts. This will help you determine the profitability of your marketing activities.

Customer acquisition cost (CAC): Determine the cost of acquiring a new customer through each marketing channel. This will help you identify the most cost-effective channels and optimize your budget allocation.

Brand awareness: Measure the level of brand awareness among your target market through surveys, social media mentions, or website traffic. This will help you assess the effectiveness of your brand-building efforts.

Regularly review and analyze your marketing KPIs to identify areas for improvement and make data-driven decisions to optimize your marketing strategy.

In conclusion, developing a marketing strategy is a critical step in promoting your innovative product or service. By understanding your target market, setting clear objectives, choosing the right marketing channels, crafting compelling messages, allocating a budget, and measuring success, you can effectively reach your target audience and drive the growth of your venture. Remember to continuously evaluate and refine your marketing strategy to stay ahead of the competition and adapt to changing market dynamics.

Building and managing your brand

B uilding a strong brand is essential for the success of any venture. Your brand is more than just a logo or a name; it is the perception and reputation of your business in the minds of your target audience. A well-managed brand can differentiate your venture from competitors, build trust with customers, and create a loyal following. In this section, we will explore the key elements of building and managing a brand that resonates with your target market.

Defining Your Brand Identity

BEFORE YOU CAN EFFECTIVELY build and manage your brand, you need to define your brand identity. Your brand identity is the unique set of characteristics, values, and attributes that distinguish your venture from others in the market. It is the foundation upon which your brand is built.

To define your brand identity, start by clearly articulating your venture's mission, vision, and values. What is the purpose of your venture? What do you aspire to achieve? What principles guide your decision-making? Answering these questions will help you establish a strong foundation for your brand.

Next, consider your target market. Who are your ideal customers? What are their needs, desires, and pain points? Understanding your target market will enable you to tailor your brand messaging and positioning to resonate with them.

Once you have a clear understanding of your mission, values, and target market, you can begin to develop your brand personality. Your brand personality is the set of human characteristics and traits that you want your brand to embody. Are you playful and fun? serious and professional? Innovative and cutting-edge? Defining your brand personality will help you create a consistent and authentic brand experience for your customers.

Crafting Your Brand Messaging

ONCE YOU HAVE DEFINED your brand identity, it's time to craft your brand messaging. Your brand messaging is the way you communicate your brand's value proposition, benefits, and unique selling points to your target audience. It should be clear, concise, and compelling.

Start by developing a brand positioning statement. This statement should succinctly describe what sets your venture apart from competitors and why customers should choose your products or services. It should highlight the key benefits and value that your venture offers.

Next, create a tagline or slogan that captures the essence of your brand. A memorable and catchy tagline can help reinforce your brand identity and make a lasting impression on your target audience.

In addition to your positioning statement and tagline, develop key messages that align with your brand identity and resonate with your target market. These messages should highlight the unique features, benefits, and value of your products or services. Use language and tone that reflect your brand personality and appeal to your target audience.

Designing Your Visual Identity

YOUR VISUAL IDENTITY plays a crucial role in building brand recognition and establishing a strong brand presence. It includes elements such as your logo, color palette, typography, and visual style.

When designing your logo, consider the key attributes and values of your brand. Choose colors, fonts, and imagery that align with your brand personality and resonate with your target audience. A well-designed logo should be simple, memorable, and versatile, allowing for easy application across various marketing materials and platforms.

In addition to your logo, establish a consistent color palette and typography that reflect your brand identity. These visual elements should be used consistently across all your marketing materials, including your website, social media profiles, packaging, and advertising.

Consider creating brand guidelines or a style guide to ensure consistency in the use of your visual identity. This document should outline the rules and specifications for using your logo, colors, fonts, and other visual elements. It will serve as a reference for anyone involved in creating marketing materials for your venture.

Building Brand Awareness and Equity

ONCE YOU HAVE DEFINED your brand identity and crafted your brand messaging, it's time to build brand awareness and equity. Brand awareness refers to the level of recognition and familiarity that your target audience has with your brand. Brand equity, on the other hand, is the perceived value and reputation of your brand in the marketplace.

To build brand awareness, leverage various marketing channels and tactics. Develop a comprehensive marketing strategy that includes online and offline initiatives. Utilize social media platforms, content marketing, search engine optimization, public relations, and advertising to reach your target audience and increase brand visibility.

Consistency is key when building brand awareness. Ensure that your brand messaging, visual identity, and tone of voice are consistent across all marketing channels and touchpoints. This consistency will help reinforce your brand identity and make a lasting impression on your target audience.

To build brand equity, focus on delivering exceptional products or services and providing a positive customer experience. Consistently deliver on your brand promise and exceed customer expectations. Encourage customer reviews and testimonials to build trust and credibility. Engage with your audience through social media and other channels to foster a sense of community and loyalty.

Managing Your Brand Reputation

MANAGING YOUR BRAND reputation is crucial for long-term success. Your brand reputation is the collective perception and opinion that people have about your venture. It is influenced by factors such as customer experiences, online reviews, media coverage, and word-of-mouth.

To effectively manage your brand reputation, monitor and respond to customer feedback and reviews. Address any negative feedback or complaints promptly and professionally. Use social listening tools to monitor mentions of your brand online and engage with your audience in a timely manner.

Proactively seek opportunities to showcase your expertise and thought leadership in your industry. Publish high-quality content, participate in industry events and conferences, and engage with relevant media outlets. Position yourself as a trusted authority in your field to enhance your brand reputation.

Finally, be transparent and authentic in your communications. Be honest about your products or services, and admit and rectify any mistakes or shortcomings. Building trust and credibility is essential for maintaining a positive brand reputation.

Building and managing your brand is a continuous process that requires careful planning, consistent execution, and ongoing monitoring. By defining your brand identity, crafting compelling brand messaging, designing a strong visual identity, building brand awareness and equity, and managing your brand reputation, you can create a powerful and memorable brand that resonates with your target audience and drives the success of your venture. Remember, your brand is not just a logo or a name; it is the embodiment of your venture's values, personality, and promise.

**Scaling and Growing
Your Venture**

Strategies for Scaling Your Business

Scaling a business is an exciting and challenging phase for any entrepreneur. It involves expanding operations, increasing revenue, and reaching a wider customer base. However, scaling a business requires careful planning, strategic decision-making, and effective execution. In this section, we will explore some key strategies for scaling your business and taking it to the next level.

Understand Your Market and Customers

BEFORE YOU CAN SCALE your business, it is crucial to have a deep understanding of your market and customers. Conduct thorough market research to identify new opportunities, trends, and customer needs. This will help you tailor your products or services to meet the demands of your target market.

Additionally, gather feedback from your existing customers to gain insights into their preferences, pain points, and expectations. This information will guide you in developing new offerings and improving your existing ones. By understanding your market and customers, you can make informed decisions and effectively allocate resources for scaling your business.

Develop a Scalable Business Model

TO SUCCESSFULLY SCALE your business, you need a scalable business model. A scalable business model is one that can handle increased demand without a proportional increase in costs. It allows you to grow your revenue while maintaining or even reducing your expenses.

Consider the following factors when developing a scalable business model:

Automation and Technology: Embrace automation and technology to streamline your operations and reduce manual work. Implementing efficient systems and processes will enable you to handle higher volumes of customers and transactions without compromising quality.

Standardization: Standardize your products, services, and processes to ensure consistency and efficiency. This will make it easier to replicate your business model in new locations or markets.

Outsourcing and Partnerships: Identify areas of your business that can be outsourced or partnered with external organizations. This can help you leverage specialized expertise, reduce costs, and focus on your core competencies.

Scalable Infrastructure: Invest in infrastructure that can support your growth. This includes scalable technology systems, production facilities, and distribution networks. Anticipate future needs and plan accordingly to avoid bottlenecks as you scale.

By developing a scalable business model, you can effectively manage growth and ensure that your business can handle increased demand.

Build a High-Performing Team

SCALING A BUSINESS requires a strong and capable team. As you grow, it is essential to attract and retain talented individuals who can contribute to your success. Here are some strategies for building a high-performing team:

Clearly Define Roles and Responsibilities: Clearly define the roles and responsibilities of each team member to avoid confusion and duplication of efforts. This will ensure that everyone understands their contribution to the overall goals of the business.

Hire for Cultural Fit: Look for individuals who align with your company's values and culture. Cultural fit is crucial for maintaining a cohesive and productive team as you scale.

Invest in Training and Development: Provide ongoing training and development opportunities for your team members. This will not only enhance their skills but also foster a culture of continuous learning and improvement.

Delegate and Empower: Delegate responsibilities and empower your team members to make decisions and take ownership of their work. This will foster a sense of ownership and accountability, allowing your business to operate efficiently even as it grows.

Foster Collaboration and Communication: Encourage collaboration and open communication within your team. This will facilitate knowledge sharing, innovation, and problem-solving, ultimately driving the success of your business.

By building a high-performing team, you can effectively manage the challenges and complexities that come with scaling your business.

Expand Your Marketing and Sales Efforts

TO SCALE YOUR BUSINESS, you need to expand your marketing and sales efforts to reach a larger audience. Here are some strategies to consider:

Target New Markets: Identify new markets or customer segments that align with your products or services. Conduct market research to understand the needs and preferences of these new markets and tailor your marketing messages accordingly.

Invest in Digital Marketing: Leverage the power of digital marketing to reach a wider audience. Develop a comprehensive online presence through search engine optimization (SEO), social media marketing, content marketing, and paid advertising.

Build Strategic Partnerships: Collaborate with complementary businesses or influencers to expand your reach. Strategic partnerships can help you tap into new customer bases and gain credibility in the market.

Refine Your Sales Process: Continuously refine and optimize your sales process to improve conversion rates. Implement sales automation tools, provide sales training to your team, and closely monitor key sales metrics.

Leverage Customer Referrals: Encourage your existing customers to refer your products or services to others. Implement a referral program that incentivizes customers to spread the word about your business.

By expanding your marketing and sales efforts, you can generate more leads, acquire new customers, and increase your revenue as you scale your business.

Monitor and Adapt

AS YOU SCALE YOUR BUSINESS, it is crucial to monitor key performance indicators (Kpis) and adapt your strategies accordingly. Regularly review and analyze your financial metrics, customer feedback, and market trends to identify areas for improvement and make informed decisions.

Be agile and willing to pivot if necessary. The business landscape is constantly evolving, and what worked in the past may not work in the future. Stay open to new opportunities, embrace innovation, and be willing to make changes to stay ahead of the competition.

In conclusion, scaling a business requires careful planning, strategic decision-making, and effective execution. By understanding your market and customers, developing a scalable business model, building a high-performing team, expanding your marketing and sales efforts, and monitoring and adapting your strategies, you can successfully scale your business and achieve long-term growth and success.

Expanding into New Markets

E xpanding into new markets is a crucial step for any entrepreneur looking to grow their venture and increase their reach. It allows you to tap into new customer segments, explore untapped opportunities, and diversify your revenue streams. However, expanding into new markets can also be challenging and requires careful planning and execution. In this section, we will explore the strategies and considerations involved in expanding into new markets.

Market Research and Analysis

BEFORE EXPANDING INTO a new market, it is essential to conduct thorough market research and analysis. This process involves gathering and analyzing data about the target market, including customer demographics, preferences, and buying behavior. By understanding the needs and wants of the new market, you can tailor your products or services to meet their specific requirements.

Market research also helps you identify potential competitors and assess the level of competition in the new market. By studying your competitors' strengths and weaknesses, you can develop strategies to differentiate your offering and gain a competitive advantage.

Additionally, market research allows you to evaluate the market size and potential demand for your products or services. This information is crucial in determining the viability and profitability of expanding into the new market.

Developing a Market Entry Strategy

ONCE YOU HAVE CONDUCTED thorough market research, the next step is to develop a market entry strategy. This strategy outlines how you will enter and establish your presence in the new market. There are several market entry strategies to consider, including:

Direct Entry

DIRECT ENTRY INVOLVES establishing a physical presence in the new market, such as opening a new branch or store. This strategy allows you to have direct control over operations and customer interactions. However, it can be costly and time-consuming, requiring significant investments in infrastructure, staffing, and marketing.

Indirect Entry

INDIRECT ENTRY INVOLVES partnering with local distributors, agents, or retailers to sell your products or services in the new market. This strategy allows you to leverage the existing networks and expertise of local partners. It can be a more cost-effective and efficient way to enter a new market, especially if you lack the resources for direct entry. However, it may also result in less control over the customer experience and brand representation.

Online Entry

ONLINE ENTRY INVOLVES expanding into a new market through e-commerce platforms or online marketplaces. This strategy allows you to reach a wide audience without the need for physical infrastructure. It can be a cost-effective and scalable way to enter new markets, especially in the digital age. However, it requires a strong online presence, effective digital marketing strategies, and a seamless customer experience.

The choice of market entry strategy depends on various factors, including your resources, target market characteristics, and competitive landscape. It is essential to carefully evaluate each option and choose the one that aligns with your business goals and capabilities.

Adapting to Cultural Differences

EXPANDING INTO NEW markets often involves entering different cultural contexts. It is crucial to understand and adapt to the cultural differences to ensure the success of your venture. Cultural differences can impact various aspects of your business, including marketing strategies, product localization, and customer service.

To effectively adapt to cultural differences, consider the following:

Language and Communication

LANGUAGE PLAYS A VITAL role in effective communication with customers and stakeholders in the new market. Translate your marketing materials, product descriptions, and customer support channels into the local language to ensure clear and accurate communication. Additionally, consider cultural nuances in communication styles and adapt your messaging accordingly.

Local Customs and Traditions

RESPECT AND UNDERSTAND the local customs and traditions to avoid cultural misunderstandings or offensive actions. Adapt your marketing campaigns, product packaging, and customer interactions to align with the cultural norms of the new market. This demonstrates your commitment to the local community and builds trust with customers.

Legal and Regulatory Considerations

EACH MARKET HAS ITS own legal and regulatory framework that businesses must comply with. Research and understand the local laws and regulations related to your industry to ensure compliance. This includes aspects such as product safety standards, intellectual property protection, and data privacy regulations.

Building Strategic Partnerships

BUILDING STRATEGIC partnerships can be instrumental in expanding into new markets. Strategic partnerships allow you to leverage the expertise, resources, and networks of established players in the new market. By collaborating with local businesses or industry leaders, you can gain access to their customer base, distribution channels, and market knowledge.

When seeking strategic partnerships, consider the following:

Complementary Offerings

LOOK FOR PARTNERS WHOSE products or services complement yours. This allows you to create synergies and offer a more comprehensive solution to customers in the new market. For example, a software company expanding into a new market could partner with a local hardware provider to offer a bundled solution.

Shared Values and Vision

CHOOSE PARTNERS WHO share similar values and vision. This ensures alignment of goals and enhances the likelihood of a successful partnership. Collaborating with partners who have a similar commitment to innovation and customer satisfaction can create a strong foundation for growth in the new market.

Trust and Reliability

ESTABLISH TRUST AND reliability with potential partners
through open communication, transparency, and delivering on
commitments. Building strong relationships based on trust is
crucial for long-term success in the new market.

Expanding into new markets is an exciting opportunity for
entrepreneurs to grow their ventures and reach new customers.
By conducting thorough market research, developing a market
entry strategy, adapting to cultural differences, and building
strategic partnerships, you can increase your chances of success
in the new market. Remember to continuously monitor and
evaluate your performance in the new market, making
necessary adjustments to ensure sustainable growth and
long-term success.

Managing Growth and Scaling Challenges

Scaling a business is an exciting and challenging phase for any entrepreneur. It is a time when your innovative ideas and hard work start to pay off, and your venture begins to grow rapidly. However, with growth comes a new set of challenges that need to be managed effectively to ensure the long-term success of your business. In this section, we will explore the key strategies and considerations for managing growth and scaling challenges.

Understanding the Growth Process

BEFORE DIVING INTO the strategies for managing growth, it is important to understand the growth process itself. Growth is not a linear path but rather a series of stages that a business goes through. These stages can be broadly categorized as follows:

Start-up Stage: This is the initial phase of your venture, where you are focused on developing and launching your innovative product or service. During this stage, you are primarily concerned with establishing a customer base and generating revenue.

Growth Stage: Once your business gains traction and starts generating consistent revenue, you enter the growth stage. This is a critical phase where you need to scale your operations, expand your customer base, and increase your market share.

Expansion Stage: In the expansion stage, your business has achieved a significant level of growth and is ready to expand into new markets or geographical locations. This stage requires careful planning and execution to ensure successful expansion.

Maturity Stage: The maturity stage is characterized by a stable and established business. At this point, your focus shifts towards sustaining your market position, optimizing operations, and exploring new opportunities for innovation.

Understanding these stages is crucial because each stage presents unique challenges and requires different strategies for managing growth effectively.

Key Strategies for Managing Growth

MANAGING GROWTH AND scaling challenges requires a proactive and strategic approach. Here are some key strategies to consider:

Develop a Scalable Business Model

TO EFFECTIVELY MANAGE growth, it is essential to have a scalable business model. A scalable business model is one that can accommodate increased demand without significant increases in costs or resources. This can be achieved by leveraging technology, automation, and efficient processes. By developing a scalable business model, you can ensure that your operations can handle the increased volume and complexity that comes with growth.

Build a strong and agile team.

AS YOUR BUSINESS GROWS, so does the need for a strong and agile team. It is important to hire talented individuals who are aligned with your vision and values. Additionally, fostering a culture of continuous learning and adaptability will enable your team to navigate the challenges that come with growth. Empower your team to take ownership of their roles and provide them with the necessary resources and support to excel.

Establish clear processes and systems.

CLEAR PROCESSES AND systems are essential for managing growth effectively. As your business expands, it becomes increasingly important to have standardized processes in place to ensure consistency and efficiency. Documenting workflows, implementing project management tools, and establishing communication channels will help streamline operations and enable effective collaboration within your team.

Monitor Key Performance Indicators (KPIs)

TO EFFECTIVELY MANAGE growth, it is crucial to monitor and measure key performance indicators (KPIs). KPIs provide valuable insights into the health and performance of your business. By tracking metrics such as revenue growth, customer acquisition costs, customer retention rates, and profitability, you can identify areas that require improvement and make data-driven decisions to drive growth.

Foster Strategic Partnerships

STRATEGIC PARTNERSHIPS can play a vital role in managing growth and scaling challenges. Collaborating with complementary businesses or industry leaders can provide access to new markets, resources, and expertise. Look for opportunities to form strategic alliances that can help accelerate your growth and expand your reach.

Invest in Technology and Innovation

AS YOUR BUSINESS GROWS, investing in technology and innovation becomes increasingly important. Embracing digital transformation and leveraging emerging technologies can help streamline operations, improve efficiency, and enhance the customer experience. Stay updated with the latest trends and advancements in your industry, and be willing to adopt new technologies that can give you a competitive edge.

Overcoming Scaling Challenges

WHILE SCALING YOUR business can be exciting, it also comes with its fair share of challenges. Here are some common scaling challenges and strategies to overcome them:

Managing Cash Flow

RAPID GROWTH CAN PUT a strain on your cash flow, especially if you are investing heavily in expansion and hiring. It is crucial to closely monitor your cash flow and ensure that you have sufficient working capital to support your growth. Consider implementing cash flow forecasting, negotiating favorable payment terms with suppliers, and exploring financing options to manage cash flow effectively.

Maintaining Quality and Customer Satisfaction

AS YOUR BUSINESS GROWS, maintaining the same level of quality and customer satisfaction can become challenging. It is important to prioritize quality control and customer service to ensure that your customers continue to have a positive experience. Implement robust quality assurance processes, invest in training your team, and actively seek customer feedback to identify areas for improvement.

Scaling Operations and Infrastructure

SCALING YOUR OPERATIONS and infrastructure is a critical aspect of managing growth. Ensure that your systems, processes, and infrastructure can handle the increased volume and complexity that comes with growth. Consider automating repetitive tasks, upgrading your technology infrastructure, and optimizing your supply chain to support scalability.

Retaining Company Culture

MAINTAINING A STRONG company culture becomes more challenging as your business grows. It is important to preserve the core values and beliefs that have contributed to your success. Communicate your vision and values consistently, involve employees in decision-making processes, and foster a sense of belonging and purpose within your team.

Balancing Innovation and Stability

AS YOUR BUSINESS SCALES, it is important to strike a balance between innovation and stability. While innovation is crucial for continued growth, stability and consistency are equally important for maintaining customer trust and operational efficiency. Foster a culture that encourages innovation while ensuring that your core business operations remain stable and reliable.

Managing growth and scaling challenges requires a combination of strategic planning, effective execution, and continuous learning. By understanding the growth process, implementing key strategies, and overcoming scaling challenges, you can position your venture for long-term success in the ever-evolving business landscape.

Building strategic partnerships

Building strategic partnerships is a crucial aspect of scaling and growing your venture. As an entrepreneur, you cannot do everything on your own, and forming alliances with other organizations can provide numerous benefits. Strategic partnerships can help you access new markets, expand your customer base, enhance your product offerings, and increase your overall competitiveness. In this section, we will explore the importance of building strategic partnerships and provide practical tips on how to establish and maintain successful collaborations.

Understanding the Value of Strategic Partnerships

STRATEGIC PARTNERSHIPS are mutually beneficial relationships between two or more organizations that work together to achieve common goals. These partnerships can take various forms, such as joint ventures, licensing agreements, distribution agreements, or co-marketing initiatives. The key to a successful strategic partnership lies in finding the right partner who shares your vision and complements your strengths and weaknesses.

One of the primary benefits of strategic partnerships is the ability to leverage each other's resources and expertise. By collaborating with another organization, you can tap into their knowledge, skills, and networks, which can significantly accelerate your growth. For example, if you are a technology startup, partnering with an established company in your industry can provide you with access to their customer base and distribution channels, giving you a competitive advantage.

Strategic partnerships also allow you to share the risks and costs associated with expanding into new markets or developing new products. By pooling your resources with a partner, you can reduce the financial burden and increase your chances of success. Additionally, partnerships can provide opportunities for innovation and co-creation, as you can combine your strengths to develop new and improved solutions that neither party could have achieved alone.

Finding the Right Strategic Partners

FINDING THE RIGHT STRATEGIC partners requires careful consideration and research. Here are some steps to help you identify potential partners:

Define your objectives: Before seeking partnerships, clearly define your goals and what you hope to achieve through collaboration. This will help you identify organizations that align with your vision and mission.

Research the market: Conduct market research to identify potential partners who operate in your target market or have expertise in areas that complement your business. Look for organizations that share similar values and have a track record of success.

Evaluate compatibility: Assess the compatibility of potential partners by considering factors such as their culture, values, and strategic direction. It is essential to find partners who have a similar mindset and are willing to invest time and resources into the partnership.

Assess capabilities: Evaluate the capabilities and resources of potential partners to ensure they can contribute effectively to the partnership. Look for organizations with complementary strengths that can enhance your competitive advantage.

Establish trust: Building trust is crucial in any partnership. Take the time to get to know potential partners and establish open and transparent communication channels. Trust is the foundation for a successful collaboration.

Establishing and Maintaining Successful Partnerships

ONCE YOU HAVE IDENTIFIED potential partners, the next step is to establish and maintain successful partnerships. Here are some key considerations:

Clearly define roles and expectations: Clearly define the roles and responsibilities of each partner to avoid misunderstandings and conflicts. Establish clear expectations regarding the goals, timelines, and deliverables of the partnership.

Develop a shared vision: Work together with your partners to develop a shared vision for the partnership. Align your goals and objectives to ensure that everyone is working towards a common purpose.

Communicate effectively: Effective communication is essential for the success of any partnership. Establish regular communication channels and ensure that all partners are kept informed about progress, challenges, and opportunities.

Foster collaboration and innovation: Encourage collaboration and innovation within the partnership. Create an environment that promotes the exchange of ideas and the co-creation of new solutions. Foster a culture of trust, openness, and creativity.

Monitor and evaluate the partnership: Regularly monitor and evaluate the progress of the partnership. Assess whether the partnership is meeting its objectives and identify areas for improvement. Make adjustments as necessary to ensure the partnership remains successful.

Nurture the relationship: Building strong relationships with your partners is crucial for long-term success. Invest time and effort in nurturing the relationship, and look for opportunities to add value to your partners. Celebrate successes together and support each other during challenging times.

Case Study: Strategic Partnerships in Action

TO ILLUSTRATE THE POWER of strategic partnerships, let's look at a real-life example. In 2014, Apple and IBM formed a strategic partnership to develop business applications for iOS devices. Apple brought its expertise in consumer technology and design, while IBM provided its deep knowledge of enterprise software and services.

The partnership allowed Apple to expand its presence in the enterprise market, which was traditionally dominated by Microsoft and other competitors. IBM, on the other hand, gained access to Apple's vast customer base and distribution channels. Together, they developed a range of industry-specific applications that transformed how businesses operate and increased productivity.

The Apple-IBM partnership demonstrates how strategic collaborations can leverage the strengths of each partner to create innovative solutions and access new markets. By combining their resources and expertise, both companies were able to achieve more significant success than they could have individually.

Building strategic partnerships is a critical step in scaling and growing your venture. By collaborating with the right partners, you can access new markets, enhance your product offerings, and increase your overall competitiveness. Remember to carefully evaluate potential partners, establish clear roles and expectations, foster effective communication, and nurture the relationship for long-term success. Strategic partnerships have the potential to unleash the full potential of your entrepreneurial mindset and drive innovation in your venture.

Innovation
in a Changing World

Adapting to Technological Advancements

In today's rapidly changing world, technological advancements are transforming industries and reshaping the way businesses operate. As an entrepreneur, it is crucial to adapt to these advancements to stay competitive and seize new opportunities for innovation. This section will explore the importance of adapting to technological advancements and provide strategies for incorporating them into your venture.

Embracing Technological Disruption

TECHNOLOGICAL ADVANCEMENTS have the power to disrupt traditional industries and create new markets. Embracing these disruptions can lead to significant growth and success for your venture. It is essential to stay informed about emerging technologies and understand how they can impact your industry.

One way to embrace technological disruption is by actively seeking out new technologies and evaluating their potential impact on your business. This can involve attending industry conferences, networking with experts, and staying up-to-date with the latest research and trends. By proactively seeking out information, you can identify opportunities for innovation and stay ahead of the curve.

Integrating Technology into Your Operations

ADAPTING TO TECHNOLOGICAL advancements requires integrating technology into your operations effectively. This involves identifying areas where technology can streamline processes, improve efficiency, and enhance the overall customer experience.

One area where technology can have a significant impact is in data analysis and decision-making. By leveraging data analytics tools, you can gain valuable insights into customer behavior, market trends, and operational efficiency. These insights can inform strategic decision-making and help you identify areas for improvement and innovation.

Another way to integrate technology into your operations is by automating repetitive tasks. This can free up time and resources, allowing you to focus on more strategic initiatives. Automation can range from simple tasks like email marketing automation to more complex processes like supply chain management.

Embracing Digital Transformation

DIGITAL TRANSFORMATION refers to the integration of digital technologies into all aspects of a business, fundamentally changing how it operates and delivers value to customers. Embracing digital transformation is essential for staying competitive in today's digital age.

To embrace digital transformation, start by assessing your current digital capabilities and identifying areas for improvement. This can involve upgrading your IT infrastructure, implementing new software systems, or adopting cloud-based solutions. By investing in digital technologies, you can enhance your operational efficiency, improve customer experiences, and unlock new revenue streams.

Additionally, digital transformation requires a shift in mindset and culture within your organization. It is crucial to foster a culture of innovation and encourage employees to embrace new technologies and adapt to change. This can involve providing training and development opportunities, creating cross-functional teams, and promoting a culture of experimentation and learning.

Leveraging Emerging Technologies

AS AN ENTREPRENEUR, it is essential to stay informed about emerging technologies and their potential impact on your industry. Emerging technologies such as artificial intelligence, blockchain, virtual reality, and the Internet of Things have the potential to revolutionize various sectors.

To leverage emerging technologies, start by conducting research and understanding how they can be applied to your business. This can involve exploring case studies, attending industry events, and networking with experts in the field. By understanding the capabilities and limitations of emerging technologies, you can identify opportunities for innovation and gain a competitive advantage.

Once you have identified a relevant emerging technology, consider piloting it in a controlled environment to assess its feasibility and potential impact. This can involve partnering with technology providers, conducting small-scale experiments, and gathering feedback from customers and employees. By taking a strategic and iterative approach, you can minimize risks and maximize the benefits of adopting emerging technologies.

Overcoming Technological Challenges

WHILE TECHNOLOGICAL advancements offer numerous opportunities for innovation, they also present challenges that entrepreneurs must overcome. Some common challenges include the cost of implementing new technologies, the need for specialized skills and expertise, and the potential for resistance to change within the organization.

To overcome these challenges, it is crucial to develop a clear technology roadmap and budget. This involves identifying the technologies that are most critical to your business and prioritizing their implementation based on their potential impact and feasibility. By taking a strategic approach, you can allocate resources effectively and minimize the financial burden of adopting new technologies.

Additionally, investing in training and development programs can help your employees acquire the skills and expertise needed to leverage new technologies. This can involve providing workshops, online courses, or partnering with educational institutions. By empowering your employees with the necessary knowledge and skills, you can ensure a smooth transition to new technologies and maximize their potential benefits.

Finally, addressing resistance to change requires effective communication and change management strategies. It is essential to involve employees in the decision-making process, communicate the benefits of adopting new technologies, and provide ongoing support and training. By fostering a culture of openness and collaboration, you can overcome resistance and create a positive environment for technological advancements.

In conclusion, adapting to technological advancements is crucial for entrepreneurs looking to stay competitive and drive innovation. By embracing technological disruption, integrating technology into operations, embracing digital transformation, leveraging emerging technologies, and overcoming technological challenges, entrepreneurs can unlock new opportunities and achieve long-term success. Embracing technological advancements is not only about keeping up with the latest trends but also about leveraging technology to create value for customers and drive sustainable growth.

Navigating disruptive changes

In today's rapidly evolving business landscape, disruptive changes have become the norm rather than the exception. Technological advancements, shifting consumer preferences, and global economic shifts are just a few examples of the forces that can disrupt industries and create both challenges and opportunities for entrepreneurs. Navigating these disruptive changes requires a combination of adaptability, foresight, and strategic decision-making. In this section, we will explore strategies and approaches that can help entrepreneurs successfully navigate disruptive changes and position their ventures for long-term success.

Embracing Change as an Opportunity

DISRUPTIVE CHANGES can be intimidating, but they also present unique opportunities for entrepreneurs who are willing to embrace them. Rather than resisting or fearing change, successful entrepreneurs view it as a chance to innovate and differentiate themselves from their competitors. They understand that change creates gaps in the market that can be filled with new and innovative solutions.

To embrace change as an opportunity, entrepreneurs must cultivate a mindset that is open to new ideas and willing to take calculated risks. They must be willing to challenge the status quo and question existing assumptions. By doing so, they can identify emerging trends and disruptions early on and position their ventures to capitalize on them.

Anticipating and Monitoring Disruptive Trends

TO NAVIGATE DISRUPTIVE changes effectively, entrepreneurs must be proactive in anticipating and monitoring trends that have the potential to impact their industries. This requires staying informed about technological advancements, market shifts, and regulatory changes that may affect their ventures.

Entrepreneurs can stay ahead of the curve by actively engaging in industry networks, attending conferences and trade shows, and participating in relevant online communities. By doing so, they can gain valuable insights into emerging trends and connect with other innovators who may be experiencing similar challenges or opportunities.

Additionally, entrepreneurs should establish a system for monitoring and analyzing market data and industry reports. This can help them identify patterns and trends that may signal disruptive changes on the horizon. By staying informed and proactive, entrepreneurs can position their ventures to adapt and thrive in the face of disruption.

Agility and Flexibility in Decision-Making

DISRUPTIVE CHANGES often require entrepreneurs to make quick and decisive decisions. In such dynamic environments, agility and flexibility are key attributes for successful entrepreneurs. They must be able to adapt their strategies and business models in response to changing market conditions.

To cultivate agility and flexibility, entrepreneurs should foster a culture of experimentation and learning within their ventures. This involves encouraging employees to take calculated risks, learn from failures, and iterate on their ideas. By embracing a mindset of continuous improvement, entrepreneurs can quickly adjust their strategies and tactics to navigate disruptive changes effectively.

Furthermore, entrepreneurs should be willing to pivot their business models if necessary. This may involve reevaluating their value proposition, target market, or distribution channels to better align with the changing landscape. By being open to change and willing to make bold decisions, entrepreneurs can position their ventures for success in the face of disruption.

Building Strategic Partnerships

NAVIGATING DISRUPTIVE changes often requires entrepreneurs to leverage external resources and expertise. Building strategic partnerships can provide access to new markets, technologies, and resources that can help entrepreneurs adapt and thrive in the face of disruption.

Strategic partnerships can take various forms, including collaborations with other businesses, joint ventures, or alliances with industry associations or research institutions. By partnering with organizations that have complementary strengths and capabilities, entrepreneurs can pool resources and knowledge to navigate disruptive changes more effectively.

When seeking strategic partnerships, entrepreneurs should look for organizations that share their vision and values. They should also consider the long-term potential of the partnership and how it aligns with their overall business strategy. By carefully selecting and nurturing strategic partnerships, entrepreneurs can enhance their ability to navigate disruptive changes and drive innovation within their ventures.

Continuous Learning and Adaptation

IN A RAPIDLY CHANGING business environment, continuous learning and adaptation are essential for entrepreneurs. They must be willing to acquire new knowledge and skills, stay updated on industry trends, and adapt their strategies accordingly.

Entrepreneurs can foster a culture of continuous learning within their ventures by encouraging employees to pursue professional development opportunities, attend industry conferences, and engage in ongoing training. By investing in their own learning and the learning of their team members, entrepreneurs can ensure that their ventures remain agile and adaptable in the face of disruptive changes.

Additionally, entrepreneurs should actively seek feedback from customers, employees, and other stakeholders. This feedback can provide valuable insights into areas for improvement and help entrepreneurs identify potential blind spots or challenges that may arise from disruptive changes. By remaining open to feedback and actively seeking input from others, entrepreneurs can make more informed decisions and navigate disruptive changes more effectively.

Navigating disruptive changes is a critical skill for entrepreneurs who want to build successful ventures in today's rapidly evolving business landscape. By embracing change as an opportunity, anticipating and monitoring disruptive trends, cultivating agility and flexibility in decision-making, building strategic partnerships, and fostering a culture of continuous learning and adaptation, entrepreneurs can position their ventures for long-term success. While disruptive changes may present challenges, they also offer unique opportunities for innovation and growth. By adopting the right mindset and implementing effective strategies, entrepreneurs can navigate disruptive changes with confidence and unlock their full potential as innovators.

Embracing Sustainability and Social Responsibility

In today's rapidly changing world, it is becoming increasingly important for entrepreneurs and businesses to embrace sustainability and social responsibility. The traditional focus on profit and growth is no longer enough to ensure long-term success. Consumers are becoming more conscious of the impact their purchasing decisions have on the environment and society, and they are actively seeking out businesses that align with their values.

The Importance of Sustainability

SUSTAINABILITY REFERS to the ability to meet the needs of the present without compromising the ability of future generations to meet their own needs. It involves considering the environmental, social, and economic impacts of business activities and making decisions that minimize harm and maximize positive outcomes. Embracing sustainability is not only the right thing to do, but it also makes good business sense.

By adopting sustainable practices, entrepreneurs can reduce their environmental footprint, conserve resources, and minimize waste. This not only helps protect the planet but also reduces costs and improves operational efficiency. Sustainable businesses are also more attractive to consumers, who are increasingly seeking out eco-friendly products and services. By positioning your venture as a sustainable and responsible business, you can tap into a growing market of environmentally conscious consumers.

Social Responsibility and Ethical Business Practices

IN ADDITION TO SUSTAINABILITY, social responsibility is another key aspect that entrepreneurs should embrace. Social responsibility refers to the ethical obligations businesses have towards society, including their employees, customers, and the communities in which they operate. It involves conducting business in a way that benefits society as a whole and goes beyond simply maximizing profits.

Entrepreneurs can demonstrate social responsibility by treating their employees fairly and providing a safe and inclusive work environment. This includes offering competitive wages, providing opportunities for growth and development, and promoting diversity and inclusion. By investing in their employees' well-being and professional development, entrepreneurs can create a motivated and engaged workforce that is more likely to contribute to the success of the venture.

Furthermore, entrepreneurs should also consider the impact their products and services have on consumers. This includes ensuring the safety and quality of their offerings, as well as being transparent about their sourcing and production processes. By prioritizing the well-being of their customers, entrepreneurs can build trust and loyalty, which are essential for long-term success.

Integrating Sustainability and Social Responsibility into Your Venture

TO EFFECTIVELY EMBRACE sustainability and social responsibility, entrepreneurs need to integrate these principles into every aspect of their venture. Here are some strategies to help you get started:

Conduct a Sustainability Audit

START BY ASSESSING your current business practices and identifying areas where you can improve sustainability and social responsibility. This may involve evaluating your supply chain, energy consumption, waste management, and employee policies. By understanding your current impact, you can develop a roadmap for implementing changes and setting goals for improvement.

Adopt Sustainable Practices

IMPLEMENT SUSTAINABLE practices throughout your venture. This may include reducing energy consumption, implementing recycling programs, using eco-friendly materials, and minimizing waste. Consider partnering with suppliers and vendors who share your commitment to sustainability. By making conscious choices about your operations, you can reduce your environmental impact and inspire others to do the same.

Engage with Stakeholders

INVOLVE YOUR EMPLOYEES, customers, and other stakeholders in your sustainability and social responsibility efforts. Educate your employees about the importance of sustainability and provide training on how they can contribute. Seek feedback from your customers and incorporate their suggestions into your business practices. By engaging with your stakeholders, you can build a sense of shared responsibility and create a positive impact together.

Collaborate with like-minded organizations.

LOOK FOR OPPORTUNITIES to collaborate with other businesses and organizations that share your commitment to sustainability and social responsibility. By partnering with like-minded organizations, you can amplify your impact and create a collective force for positive change. This may involve participating in industry associations, joining sustainability initiatives, or supporting local community projects.

Communicate Your Commitment

FINALLY, COMMUNICATE your commitment to sustainability and social responsibility to your stakeholders. This includes sharing your goals, progress, and achievements through various channels, such as your website, social media, and marketing materials. By being transparent and accountable, you can build trust and attract customers who align with your values.

The Benefits of Embracing Sustainability and Social Responsibility

EMBRACING SUSTAINABILITY and social responsibility offers numerous benefits for entrepreneurs and their ventures. Here are some of the key advantages:

Competitive Advantage

BY POSITIONING YOUR venture as a sustainable and socially responsible business, you can differentiate yourself from competitors and attract customers who prioritize these values. This can give you a competitive edge in the market and help you build a loyal customer base.

Cost Savings

IMPLEMENTING SUSTAINABLE practices can lead to cost savings in the long run. By reducing energy consumption, minimizing waste, and optimizing processes, you can lower your operational costs and improve your bottom line.

Enhanced Reputation

BEING KNOWN AS A SUSTAINABLE and socially responsible business can enhance your reputation and improve your brand image. This can lead to increased trust and credibility among customers, investors, and other stakeholders.

Attracting and Retaining Talent

IN TODAY'S COMPETITIVE job market, employees are increasingly seeking out employers who prioritize sustainability and social responsibility. By demonstrating your commitment to these values, you can attract and retain top talent who shares your vision.

Long-Term Success

EMBRACING SUSTAINABILITY and social responsibility is not just a short-term trend; it is a long-term strategy for success. By aligning your venture with the values of your customers and society, you can build a resilient and future-proof business that is well-positioned for long-term success.

In conclusion, embracing sustainability and social responsibility is not only a moral imperative but also a strategic business decision. By integrating these principles into your venture, you can create a positive impact on the environment and society while also reaping the benefits of increased customer loyalty, cost savings, and long-term success. As an entrepreneur, it is your responsibility to unleash your inner innovator and build a venture that not only drives profit but also contributes to a better and more sustainable world.

Innovation in the Digital Age

In today's rapidly evolving world, the digital age has brought about significant changes in the way we live, work, and do business. The advent of technology and the internet has revolutionized every aspect of our lives, including how we innovate. The digital age has opened up new opportunities for entrepreneurs to unleash their creativity and drive innovation in ways that were previously unimaginable.

7.4.1 Embracing Digital Transformation

DIGITAL TRANSFORMATION is the integration of digital technology into all areas of a business, fundamentally changing how it operates and delivers value to customers. Embracing digital transformation is crucial for entrepreneurs who want to stay competitive and drive innovation in the digital age. By leveraging digital tools and technologies, entrepreneurs can streamline their operations, enhance customer experiences, and create new business models.

Harnessing the Power of Data

IN THE DIGITAL AGE, data has become a valuable asset for entrepreneurs. The abundance of data available through various digital channels provides entrepreneurs with valuable insights into customer behavior, market trends, and industry dynamics. By harnessing the power of data analytics, entrepreneurs can make informed decisions, identify new opportunities, and develop innovative solutions that meet the needs of their target market.

Leveraging Artificial Intelligence and Machine Learning

ARTIFICIAL INTELLIGENCE (AI) and machine learning (ML) are revolutionizing the way businesses operate and innovate. AI and ML technologies enable entrepreneurs to automate processes, analyze vast amounts of data, and make predictions based on patterns and trends. By leveraging AI and ML, entrepreneurs can enhance their decision-making capabilities, personalize customer experiences, and develop innovative products and services.

Embracing Agile and Lean Methodologies

IN THE DIGITAL AGE, traditional business models and approaches to innovation are no longer sufficient. Entrepreneurs need to embrace agile and lean methodologies to adapt to the rapidly changing digital landscape. Agile methodologies, such as Scrum and Kanban, enable entrepreneurs to quickly iterate and respond to customer feedback, while lean methodologies, such as the Lean Startup approach, help entrepreneurs validate their ideas and minimize waste.

Fostering a Culture of Innovation

INNOVATION IN THE DIGITAL age requires a culture that fosters creativity, collaboration, and experimentation. Entrepreneurs need to create an environment where employees are encouraged to think outside the box, share ideas, and take calculated risks. By fostering a culture of innovation, entrepreneurs can unleash the full potential of their teams and drive continuous improvement and growth.

Embracing Disruption and Uncertainty

THE DIGITAL AGE IS characterized by constant disruption and uncertainty. Entrepreneurs need to embrace these challenges and view them as opportunities for innovation. By embracing disruption and uncertainty, entrepreneurs can stay ahead of the competition, identify new market trends, and develop innovative solutions that meet the evolving needs of their customers.

Leveraging Digital Marketing and Social Media

IN THE DIGITAL AGE, traditional marketing approaches are no longer sufficient. Entrepreneurs need to leverage digital marketing strategies and social media platforms to reach their target audience effectively. By utilizing digital marketing techniques such as search engine optimization (SEO), content marketing, and social media advertising, entrepreneurs can increase their brand visibility, engage with their customers, and drive innovation through effective communication and feedback.

Building Strategic Partnerships in the Digital Ecosystem

IN THE DIGITAL AGE, entrepreneurs can leverage strategic partnerships to drive innovation and accelerate growth. By collaborating with other businesses, startups, or technology providers, entrepreneurs can access new markets, technologies, and resources that can fuel their innovation efforts. Strategic partnerships enable entrepreneurs to combine their strengths, share risks, and create synergies that can lead to breakthrough innovations and long-term success.

Ensuring Cybersecurity and Data Privacy

IN THE DIGITAL AGE, cybersecurity and data privacy are critical considerations for entrepreneurs. With the increasing reliance on digital technologies and the collection of vast amounts of data, entrepreneurs need to prioritize the protection of their customers' information and ensure compliance with data privacy regulations. By implementing robust cybersecurity measures and adopting best practices for data privacy, entrepreneurs can build trust with their customers and safeguard their innovation efforts.

Adapting to the Future of Innovation

THE DIGITAL AGE IS just the beginning of a new era of innovation. As technology continues to advance at an unprecedented pace, entrepreneurs need to stay agile, adaptable, and open to new possibilities. By continuously learning, experimenting, and embracing emerging technologies, entrepreneurs can position themselves at the forefront of innovation and drive long-term success in the ever-changing digital landscape.

Innovation in the digital age is not just about embracing technology; it's about embracing a mindset of continuous improvement, adaptability, and creativity. By leveraging the power of digital tools, data, and emerging technologies, entrepreneurs can unleash their inner innovator and build successful ventures that thrive in the digital age.

Sustaining Innovation and Long-Term Success

Creating a Culture of Innovation

Innovation is not just about coming up with great ideas; it is about creating a culture that fosters and nurtures innovation. A culture of innovation is an environment where creativity, experimentation, and risk-taking are encouraged and rewarded. It is a mindset that permeates every aspect of an organization, from its leadership to its employees.

The Role of Leadership

CREATING A CULTURE of innovation starts at the top. Leaders play a crucial role in setting the tone and creating an environment that promotes innovation. They need to lead by example, demonstrating their own willingness to take risks and try new things. They should encourage and support their employees' ideas and provide them with the resources and autonomy to pursue innovative projects.

Leaders also need to communicate the importance of innovation and its alignment with the organization's goals and vision. They should articulate a clear and compelling vision for the future and inspire their teams to think creatively and push boundaries. By fostering a culture of innovation, leaders can create a sense of purpose and excitement that motivates employees to go above and beyond.

Encouraging Collaboration and Diversity

INNOVATION THRIVES in an environment that encourages collaboration and embraces diverse perspectives. When people from different backgrounds and disciplines come together, they bring unique insights and ideas that can spark innovation. Organizations should create opportunities for cross-functional collaboration and provide platforms for employees to share their ideas and collaborate on projects.

To foster collaboration, organizations can establish innovation hubs or dedicated spaces where employees can come together to brainstorm, experiment, and collaborate. These spaces should be designed to facilitate open communication and idea sharing, with tools and resources readily available to support the innovation process.

Embracing a Growth Mindset

A GROWTH MINDSET IS essential for fostering a culture of innovation. It is the belief that abilities and intelligence can be developed through dedication and hard work. In a culture with a growth mindset, failure is seen as an opportunity for learning and growth rather than a setback. Employees are encouraged to take risks, experiment, and learn from their mistakes.

Organizations can promote a growth mindset by providing opportunities for continuous learning and development. This can include training programs, workshops, and mentorship initiatives that help employees build new skills and expand their knowledge. By investing in their employees' growth and development, organizations create a culture that values learning and encourages innovation.

Rewarding and Recognizing Innovation

TO SUSTAIN A CULTURE of innovation, organizations need to reward and recognize innovative efforts. This can be done through various means, such as monetary incentives, promotions, or public recognition. By acknowledging and celebrating innovative achievements, organizations send a clear message that innovation is valued and encouraged.

In addition to tangible rewards, organizations should also create a supportive and inclusive environment where employees feel safe to share their ideas and take risks. This can be achieved by fostering a culture of psychological safety, where individuals feel comfortable expressing their opinions and challenging the status quo without fear of negative consequences.

Creating an Agile and Adaptive Organization

INNOVATION REQUIRES agility and adaptability. Organizations need to be able to respond quickly to changing market conditions, customer needs, and technological advancements. This requires a flexible and adaptive organizational structure and process.

Organizations can adopt agile methodologies, such as Scrum or Kanban, to enable faster decision-making, iterative development, and continuous improvement. These methodologies promote cross-functional collaboration, transparency, and a focus on delivering customer value. By embracing agility, organizations can create an environment that supports innovation and enables rapid experimentation and learning.

Empowering Employees

EMPOWERING EMPLOYEES is a key aspect of creating a culture of innovation. When employees feel empowered, they are more likely to take ownership of their work, think creatively, and contribute innovative ideas. Organizations can empower employees by providing them with autonomy, decision-making authority, and the resources they need to pursue innovative projects.

Leaders should trust their employees and delegate decision-making authority, allowing them to take risks and make decisions without constant supervision. This not only empowers employees but also fosters a sense of ownership and accountability. By empowering employees, organizations tap into their full potential and unleash their creativity and innovation.

Continuous Improvement and Feedback

CREATING A CULTURE of innovation requires a commitment to continuous improvement. Organizations should regularly evaluate their processes, systems, and practices to identify areas for improvement and innovation. This can be done through feedback mechanisms such as surveys, focus groups, or regular performance reviews.

Feedback should be constructive and focused on growth and improvement. It should encourage employees to reflect on their work, identify areas for development, and seek opportunities for innovation. By fostering a culture of continuous improvement, organizations create an environment that values innovation and encourages employees to strive for excellence.

Creating a culture of innovation is not a one-time event; it is an ongoing process that requires commitment, effort, and continuous improvement. By fostering a culture that encourages collaboration, embraces diversity, and rewards innovation, organizations can unleash the full potential of their employees and drive long-term success. A culture of innovation is not only essential for staying ahead of the competition but also for creating a better future through continuous innovation and improvement.

Continuous learning and adaptation

Innovation is not a one-time event; it is an ongoing process that requires continuous learning and adaptation. As an entrepreneur, it is crucial to embrace a mindset of constant growth and improvement in order to stay ahead in a rapidly changing business landscape. This chapter will explore the importance of continuous learning and adaptation in sustaining innovation and achieving long-term success.

Embracing a Growth Mindset

ONE OF THE KEY ELEMENTS of continuous learning and adaptation is embracing a growth mindset. A growth mindset is the belief that abilities and intelligence can be developed through dedication and hard work. Entrepreneurs with a growth mindset are more likely to view challenges as opportunities for growth and are willing to take risks and learn from their failures.

To cultivate a growth mindset, entrepreneurs should focus on developing a love for learning and a curiosity to explore new ideas and concepts. They should seek out opportunities for personal and professional development, such as attending workshops, conferences, and networking events. Additionally, entrepreneurs should surround themselves with like-minded individuals who can provide support and encouragement in their journey of continuous learning.

Learning from Failure

FAILURE IS AN INEVITABLE part of the entrepreneurial journey. However, instead of viewing failure as a setback, successful entrepreneurs see it as a valuable learning experience. They understand that failure provides an opportunity to reflect, learn, and adapt their strategies.

To effectively learn from failure, entrepreneurs should adopt a reflective mindset. This involves analyzing the reasons behind the failure, identifying the lessons learned, and implementing changes to avoid similar mistakes in the future. It is important to approach failure with a positive attitude and view it as a stepping stone towards success.

Embracing Change and Adaptation

IN TODAY'S FAST-PACED business environment, change is constant. Successful entrepreneurs understand the importance of embracing change and adapting their strategies to stay relevant and competitive. They are open to new ideas, technologies, and market trends and are willing to make necessary adjustments to their business models.

To effectively embrace change and adaptation, entrepreneurs should stay informed about industry trends and advancements. They should actively seek feedback from customers, employees, and industry experts to identify areas for improvement and innovation. Additionally, entrepreneurs should be flexible and agile in their decision-making process, allowing them to quickly respond to market changes and adjust their strategies accordingly.

Continuous Learning and Skill Development

CONTINUOUS LEARNING goes beyond acquiring knowledge; it also involves developing new skills and competencies. As an entrepreneur, it is important to constantly upgrade your skills to meet the evolving demands of your venture.

Entrepreneurs can engage in various learning activities to enhance their skills, such as attending workshops, taking online courses, reading industry publications, and participating in professional development programs. By continuously expanding their skill set, entrepreneurs can effectively adapt to new challenges and seize opportunities for innovation.

Building a Learning Organization

IN ADDITION TO PERSONAL growth, entrepreneurs should also focus on building a learning organization. A learning organization is one that encourages and supports continuous learning and knowledge sharing among its employees.

To create a learning organization, entrepreneurs should foster a culture of curiosity, collaboration, and experimentation. They should provide opportunities for employees to engage in training programs, attend conferences, and participate in cross-functional projects. Additionally, entrepreneurs should establish feedback mechanisms and encourage open communication to facilitate the exchange of ideas and insights.

Leveraging Technology for Learning

TECHNOLOGY PLAYS A crucial role in enabling continuous learning and adaptation. Entrepreneurs can leverage various digital tools and platforms to access a wealth of information, connect with industry experts, and collaborate with like-minded individuals.

Online learning platforms, such as e-learning courses and webinars, provide entrepreneurs with the flexibility to learn at their own pace and convenience. Social media platforms and online communities offer opportunities for networking and knowledge-sharing. Additionally, entrepreneurs can use data analytics tools to gather insights and make data-driven decisions.

The Importance of Feedback and Evaluation

CONTINUOUS LEARNING and adaptation require regular feedback and evaluation. Entrepreneurs should actively seek feedback from customers, employees, and stakeholders to gain insights into their performance and identify areas for improvement.

Feedback can be obtained through various channels, such as surveys, focus groups, and one-on-one interviews. Additionally, entrepreneurs should establish key performance indicators (KPIs) and regularly evaluate their progress towards their goals. By continuously monitoring and evaluating their performance, entrepreneurs can make informed decisions and adapt their strategies accordingly.

Collaboration and Knowledge Sharing

COLLABORATION AND KNOWLEDGE sharing are essential components of continuous learning and adaptation. Entrepreneurs should actively seek opportunities to collaborate with other individuals and organizations to exchange ideas, insights, and best practices.

Collaboration can take various forms, such as partnerships, joint ventures, and industry networks. By collaborating with others, entrepreneurs can leverage their collective knowledge and resources, accelerate their learning process, and drive innovation.

Continuous learning and adaptation are critical for sustaining innovation and achieving long-term success as an entrepreneur. By embracing a growth mindset, learning from failure, and adapting to change, entrepreneurs can stay ahead in a rapidly changing business landscape. Through continuous learning, skill development, and collaboration, entrepreneurs can build a learning organization that fosters innovation and drives long-term success.

Managing Intellectual Property

Intellectual property (IP) is a valuable asset for any innovative venture. It refers to the legal rights that protect creations of the mind, such as inventions, designs, trademarks, and copyrights. Managing intellectual property is crucial for entrepreneurs to safeguard their innovations, maintain a competitive advantage, and maximize the value of their ideas. In this section, we will explore the importance of managing intellectual property and discuss strategies for effectively protecting and leveraging it.

Understanding Intellectual Property Rights

BEFORE DELVING INTO the management of intellectual property, it is essential to understand the different types of intellectual property rights. The main categories of intellectual property include:

Patents: Patents protect inventions and provide exclusive rights to the inventor for a limited period. They prevent others from making, using, or selling the patented invention without permission. Patents are crucial for protecting technological innovations and can be obtained for new processes, products, or improvements to existing inventions.

Trademarks: Trademarks are symbols, names, or logos that distinguish a company's products or services from others in the market. They help build brand recognition and prevent others from using similar marks, which may cause confusion among consumers. Registering a trademark provides legal protection and allows entrepreneurs to enforce their rights against infringement.

Copyrights: Copyrights protect original works of authorship, such as literary, artistic, or musical creations. They grant the creator exclusive rights to reproduce, distribute, display, or perform the work. Copyrights are automatic upon creation, but registering them provides additional benefits, such as the ability to sue for infringement and claim statutory damages.

Trade Secrets: Trade secrets are valuable information that gives a business a competitive advantage. They can include formulas, processes, customer lists, or any confidential business information. Unlike patents or trademarks, trade secrets are not publicly disclosed and can be protected indefinitely, as long as they remain secret.

Understanding these different types of intellectual property rights is crucial for entrepreneurs to determine which ones are relevant to their innovations and how to best protect them.

Importance of Managing Intellectual Property

MANAGING INTELLECTUAL property is essential for several reasons:

Protection: Intellectual property protection prevents others from copying or imitating your innovations, giving you a competitive advantage in the market. It allows you to control the use and commercialization of your ideas, ensuring that you reap the benefits of your hard work and investment.

Value Creation: Intellectual property can be a significant source of value for your venture. It can attract investors, enhance your company's reputation, and provide licensing or partnership opportunities. By effectively managing your intellectual property, you can leverage it to generate revenue and increase the overall worth of your business.

Legal Compliance: Managing intellectual property ensures that you comply with the relevant laws and regulations governing intellectual property rights. Failing to protect your innovations adequately can result in infringement by others or the loss of your rights. By proactively managing your intellectual property, you can avoid legal disputes and protect your venture's interests.

Strategic Advantage: Intellectual property can be a strategic tool for gaining a competitive edge. By securing patents or trademarks, you can prevent competitors from entering your market or imitating your products. It allows you to differentiate your offerings and establish a unique position in the industry.

Strategies for Managing Intellectual Property

TO EFFECTIVELY MANAGE intellectual property, entrepreneurs should consider the following strategies:

Conduct IP Audits: Conducting regular IP audits helps identify and assess the intellectual property assets of your venture. It involves reviewing your innovations, trademarks, copyrights, and trade secrets to determine their value, legal protection, and potential risks. An IP audit enables you to identify any gaps in protection and develop strategies to address them.

File for Protection: Once you have identified the intellectual property assets that require protection, it is crucial to file for the appropriate legal protections. This may involve filing patent applications, registering trademarks, or copyrighting your creative works. Engaging with intellectual property attorneys or specialists can help ensure that the filing process is done correctly and efficiently.

Implement Confidentiality Measures: Protecting trade secrets and confidential information is vital for maintaining a competitive advantage. Implementing confidentiality agreements, restricting access to sensitive information, and establishing internal protocols for handling confidential data can help safeguard your trade secrets.

Monitor and enforce: Regularly monitoring the market for potential infringements of your intellectual property is crucial. This can be done through online searches, monitoring competitor activities, and engaging with intellectual property professionals. If infringement is detected, taking prompt legal action is essential to enforcing your rights and protecting your innovations.

Licensing and Partnerships: Licensing your intellectual property to other companies can be a lucrative revenue stream. By granting others the right to use your innovations in exchange for royalties or licensing fees, you can generate income while expanding the reach of your ideas. Additionally, strategic partnerships can help leverage your intellectual property for mutual benefit and market expansion.

International Considerations: If you plan to expand your venture globally, it is essential to consider international intellectual property protection. Different countries have varying laws and regulations regarding intellectual property rights. Engaging with intellectual property professionals who specialize in international law can help navigate the complexities of protecting your innovations in different jurisdictions.

Managing intellectual property is a critical aspect of building a successful venture. By understanding the different types of intellectual property rights, entrepreneurs can effectively protect and leverage their innovations. Implementing strategies such as conducting IP audits, filing for protection, implementing confidentiality measures, and monitoring and enforcing rights can help entrepreneurs maximize the value of their intellectual property assets. By managing intellectual property strategically, entrepreneurs can secure a competitive advantage, attract investors, and ensure the long-term success of their innovative ventures.

Staying Ahead of the Competition

I n today's fast-paced and highly competitive business landscape, staying ahead of the competition is crucial for the long-term success of any venture. As an entrepreneur and innovator, it is essential to continuously evolve and adapt to the ever-changing market dynamics. This section will explore strategies and approaches that can help you stay ahead of the competition and maintain your position as a leader in your industry.

Understanding the Competitive Landscape

TO STAY AHEAD OF THE competition, it is vital to have a deep understanding of the competitive landscape in which your venture operates. This involves conducting thorough market research and analysis to identify your competitors, their strengths and weaknesses, and their strategies. By understanding your competition, you can identify gaps and opportunities that can be leveraged to gain a competitive advantage.

Differentiation and Unique Value Proposition

ONE OF THE MOST EFFECTIVE ways to stay ahead of the competition is by differentiating your venture and offering a unique value proposition to your target market. This involves identifying what sets your product or service apart from others in the market and communicating that value to your customers. By offering something unique and valuable, you can attract and retain customers, even in the face of intense competition.

Continuous Innovation and Improvement

INNOVATION IS THE LIFEBLOOD of any successful venture. To stay ahead of the competition, it is crucial to foster a culture of continuous innovation and improvement within your organization. This involves encouraging creativity and idea generation, embracing new technologies and trends, and constantly seeking ways to enhance your products, services, and processes. By continuously innovating and improving, you can stay ahead of the competition and meet the evolving needs of your customers.

Embracing Technology and Digital Transformation

IN TODAY'S DIGITAL age, technology plays a significant role in shaping the competitive landscape. To stay ahead of the competition, it is essential to embrace technology and leverage it to your advantage. This can involve adopting new digital tools and platforms, implementing automation and artificial intelligence, and utilizing data analytics to gain insights and make informed business decisions. By embracing technology and digital transformation, you can streamline your operations, enhance customer experiences, and gain a competitive edge.

Building Strategic Partnerships

COLLABORATION AND STRATEGIC partnerships can be powerful tools for staying ahead of the competition. By partnering with other organizations that complement your strengths and fill your gaps, you can access new markets, technologies, and resources. Strategic partnerships can also help you leverage the expertise and networks of your partners, enabling you to innovate and grow more effectively. By building strategic partnerships, you can expand your reach, enhance your capabilities, and stay ahead of the competition.

Continuous Monitoring and Adaptation

TO STAY AHEAD OF THE competition, it is crucial to continuously monitor the market, industry trends, and customer preferences. This involves gathering and analyzing data, tracking competitors' activities, and staying informed about emerging technologies and market disruptions. By staying vigilant and adaptable, you can proactively respond to changes in the market and adjust your strategies and offerings accordingly. Continuous monitoring and adaptation allow you to stay ahead of the competition and seize new opportunities as they arise.

Investing in Talent and Skills Development

THE SUCCESS OF ANY venture relies heavily on the skills and capabilities of its workforce. To stay ahead of the competition, it is essential to invest in talent acquisition and development. This involves attracting and retaining top talent, providing ongoing training and development opportunities, and fostering a culture of learning and growth. By investing in talent and skill development, you can build a high-performing team that can drive innovation and help you maintain a competitive advantage.

Customer-Centric Approach

IN TODAY'S CUSTOMER-centric business environment, understanding and meeting the needs of your customers is paramount. To stay ahead of the competition, it is crucial to adopt a customer-centric approach in all aspects of your venture. This involves actively listening to your customers, gathering feedback, and continuously improving your products, services, and customer experiences. By putting your customers at the center of your business, you can build strong relationships, foster loyalty, and differentiate yourself from the competition.

Agility and Speed

IN A RAPIDLY CHANGING business landscape, agility and speed are essential for staying ahead of the competition. Being able to quickly adapt to market changes, customer demands, and emerging trends can give you a significant competitive advantage. This requires a flexible and responsive organizational structure, streamlined decision-making processes, and a willingness to take calculated risks. By being agile and fast-moving, you can seize opportunities, outmaneuver competitors, and stay ahead of the game.

Continuous Competitive Analysis

FINALLY, TO STAY AHEAD of the competition, it is crucial to conduct continuous competitive analysis. This involves regularly evaluating your competitors' strategies, offerings, and performance to identify areas where you can improve and differentiate yourself. By staying informed about your competition, you can anticipate their moves, identify potential threats, and proactively respond to changes in the market. Continuous competitive analysis allows you to stay ahead of the competition and maintain your position as a leader in your industry.

In conclusion, staying ahead of the competition requires a combination of strategic thinking, continuous innovation, and a customer-centric approach. By understanding the competitive landscape, differentiating your venture, embracing technology, building strategic partnerships, and continuously monitoring and adapting to market changes, you can stay ahead of the competition and achieve long-term success. Remember, the business landscape is constantly evolving, and staying ahead requires a commitment to continuous learning, improvement, and adaptation.

Measuring and Evaluating Innovation Success

Measuring and evaluating the success of innovation is crucial for any venture. It allows entrepreneurs to assess the effectiveness of their innovative ideas, strategies, and processes. By understanding how to measure and evaluate innovation success, entrepreneurs can make informed decisions, identify areas for improvement, and ensure the long-term sustainability of their ventures.

Key Performance Indicators (Kpis)

ONE OF THE PRIMARY ways to measure and evaluate innovation success is through the use of key performance indicators (KPIs). KPIs are quantifiable metrics that help entrepreneurs track and assess the performance of their innovation efforts. By setting specific KPIs, entrepreneurs can measure the progress and impact of their innovative ideas.

When selecting KPIs, it is essential to align them with the goals and objectives of the venture. Some common KPIs for measuring innovation success include:

Revenue Growth: This KPI measures the increase in revenue generated by innovative products or services. It provides insights into market acceptance and demand for the innovation.

Customer Acquisition and Retention: This KPI measures the number of new customers acquired and the rate at which existing customers are retained. It indicates the effectiveness of the innovation in attracting and retaining customers.

Time to Market: This KPI measures the time it takes to bring an innovative product or service to market. It reflects the efficiency of the innovation process and the ability to respond quickly to market needs.

Return on Investment (ROI): This KPI measures the financial return generated by the innovation compared to the investment made. It helps entrepreneurs assess the profitability and viability of their innovative ideas.

Employee Engagement and Satisfaction: This KPI measures the level of employee engagement and satisfaction within the venture. It indicates the impact of innovation on the overall work environment and culture.

Market Share: This KPI measures the percentage of the market that the venture captures with its innovative products or services. It provides insights into the competitiveness and market penetration of the innovation.

Intellectual Property (IP) Portfolio: This KPI measures the number and quality of intellectual property assets generated through the innovation process. It reflects the ability to protect and leverage innovation for future growth.

By regularly tracking and analyzing these KPIs, entrepreneurs can gain a comprehensive understanding of the success and impact of their innovation efforts.

Innovation Metrics and Tools

IN ADDITION TO KPIS, entrepreneurs can utilize various innovation metrics and tools to measure and evaluate innovation success. These metrics and tools provide more specific insights into different aspects of the innovation process. Some commonly used innovation metrics and tools include:

Idea Conversion Rate: This metric measures the percentage of ideas that successfully progress from the ideation stage to implementation. It helps entrepreneurs assess the effectiveness of their idea-generation and selection processes.

Innovation Pipeline: This tool visualizes the flow of innovative ideas through different stages of the innovation process. It allows entrepreneurs to identify bottlenecks and optimize the efficiency of the innovation pipeline.

Customer Feedback and Surveys: Collecting feedback from customers through surveys and interviews provides valuable insights into the satisfaction and perception of innovative products or services. It helps entrepreneurs understand the customer's perspective and make necessary improvements.

Innovation Index: This metric measures the overall innovation performance of the venture. It takes into account various factors, such as revenue growth, market share, and employee engagement, to provide a holistic view of innovation success.

Innovation Portfolio Analysis: This tool assesses the composition and performance of the venture's innovation portfolio. It helps entrepreneurs identify high-potential innovations and allocate resources effectively.

Benchmarking: Benchmarking involves comparing the venture's innovation performance against industry peers or competitors. It provides a benchmark for evaluating the relative success of innovation efforts.

Innovation Culture Assessment: This tool assesses the strength and effectiveness of the venture's innovation culture. It helps entrepreneurs identify areas for improvement and foster a culture that supports innovation.

By leveraging these innovation metrics and tools, entrepreneurs can gain deeper insights into the success and impact of their innovation efforts. They can identify strengths, weaknesses, and areas for improvement, enabling them to make data-driven decisions and drive continuous innovation.

Continuous Improvement and Adaptation

MEASURING AND EVALUATING innovation success is not a one-time activity. It is an ongoing process that requires continuous improvement and adaptation. As the venture evolves and the market changes, entrepreneurs need to reassess their KPIs, metrics, and tools to ensure they remain relevant and effective.

Regularly reviewing and analyzing the data collected from measuring and evaluating innovation success allows entrepreneurs to identify trends, patterns, and areas for improvement. It enables them to adapt their strategies, processes, and products to meet changing market needs and stay ahead of the competition.

Moreover, entrepreneurs should foster a culture of continuous learning and experimentation within their ventures. Encouraging employees to share their insights, ideas, and feedback can lead to valuable innovations and improvements. By embracing a growth mindset and being open to feedback, entrepreneurs can create an environment that supports innovation and drives long-term success.

Measuring and evaluating innovation success is essential for entrepreneurs to assess the effectiveness of their innovative ideas and strategies. By utilizing KPIs, innovation metrics, and tools, entrepreneurs can gain valuable insights into the impact of their innovation efforts. Continuous improvement and adaptation are key to sustaining innovation and ensuring long-term success. By fostering a culture of innovation and embracing a growth mindset, entrepreneurs can unleash their inner innovator and build successful ventures.

Also by imed el arbi

**Metamorphosis Mindset: Transforming Your Life, One
Thought at a Time**
Life Mastery: a Toolkit for Success
Your Hidden Power of Mind: Unleashing Your Full Potential
Rise to Radiance
Realize Your Ultimate Potential
Revitalize Your Reality: The Art of Life Transformation
Transforming Within: A Path to Personal Evolution

YouTube Secrets
YouTube Secrets: Build a Successful Channel in 5 Days
YouTube Secrets: Build a Successful Channel with Artificial
Intelligence
YouTube Secrets: the Ultimate Guide to Creating Popular and
Successful Content

Standalone
The Magical Woodland Adventure

The Secret Garden of Whispers
Timmy's Savanna Adventure
The Fisherman's Destiny
The Gathering in the Forest
The Great Adventure of a Lost Teddy
The Dinosaur Who Travels Through Time
The most beautiful stories for children
Felix's Lesson: The Love We Share
Luna the Moonchild's Dreamland Adventure
Sophie's Wish on the Wishing Star
The Adventure in the Enchanted Forest
Discover the Better Self Secret
Discover the Better Self Secret
ThePrincess and the Dragon's Surprising Bond
Blogging Manual for Beginner's
Lily and the Pixie: A Story of Kindness and Compassion
The Magic Portal
Whisker's Great Journey
Becoming Creative: The Path to Expressive Living
Elinor's Radiant Victory
Financial Amplification:How to Make More Money
Unique Discoveries in Tunisia
Mastering Your Mental Health
Chasing Dreams and Finding Magic
Habit Revolution: Mastering the Art of Building Good
Habits and Breaking Bad Ones
WordPress Mastery: Your Ultimate Website Guide
Money Mindset: How to Reprogram Your Brain for Financial
Success
Breaking Free: Uncovering Your Money Mindset

The Money Mindset Makeover: Unleashing True Financial Potential
Digital Deception: A Detective Jane Miller Mystery
The Enigma of Slytherin's Legacy
Bound by Love and Betrayal: an Immigrant's Journey
Tesla's 369 Revelation: A Journey to Spiritual Power
Silencing the Inner Critic: Unleashing Your True Potential
Smoke-Free Success: a Path to Health and Wealth
Navigating Success: 7 Principles of High Achievers
Charm 101: the Art of Wooing Women
Motivate Your Mind:Mastering Motivation for Success
Enchanting Cities: Exploring the World's Urban Treasures
How to Build a Successful Career in the Gig Economy
Mindful Living in the Digital Era
Raising Resilient Kids: a Mindful Guide to Parenting
The Compassionate Self: Cultivating Kindness Within
The Science of Happiness: The Pursuit of Joy
Freelance Writing Success: Launch, Grow, and Scale Your Career
Emotional Well-being: A Guide to Mental Health
HABITS RICH PEOPLE WON'T TELL YOU
Rich Habits, Rich Life: Mastering the Art of Wealth Building
Rising Horizons: Accelerating Business Development
The Lost City of Mythica: Uncovering Mythica's Secret
Generational Harmony: Winning Through Diversity
Alchemy of the Soul: A Roadmap to Life Transformation
Rise Strong: Embracing Resilience and Renewal
AI Riches: Unleashing the Profit Potential of Artificial Intelligence
Building Your Online Store with WooCommerce
Online Entrepreneurship: Success Roadmap

Attracting Success: Unlocking the Hidden Forces of the Law of Attraction

Wellness and Safety: A Guide to Health and Care

The Last Queen of Egypt: A Tale of Power, Love, and Legacy

The Entrepreneurial Mindset: Building Success